CANNING

MEAT COOKBOOK

FOR BEGINNERS

Preserve Your Meat and Game Safely | Delicious and Affordable Traditional Recipes for Long-Term Pantry Staples

Olivia A. Morris

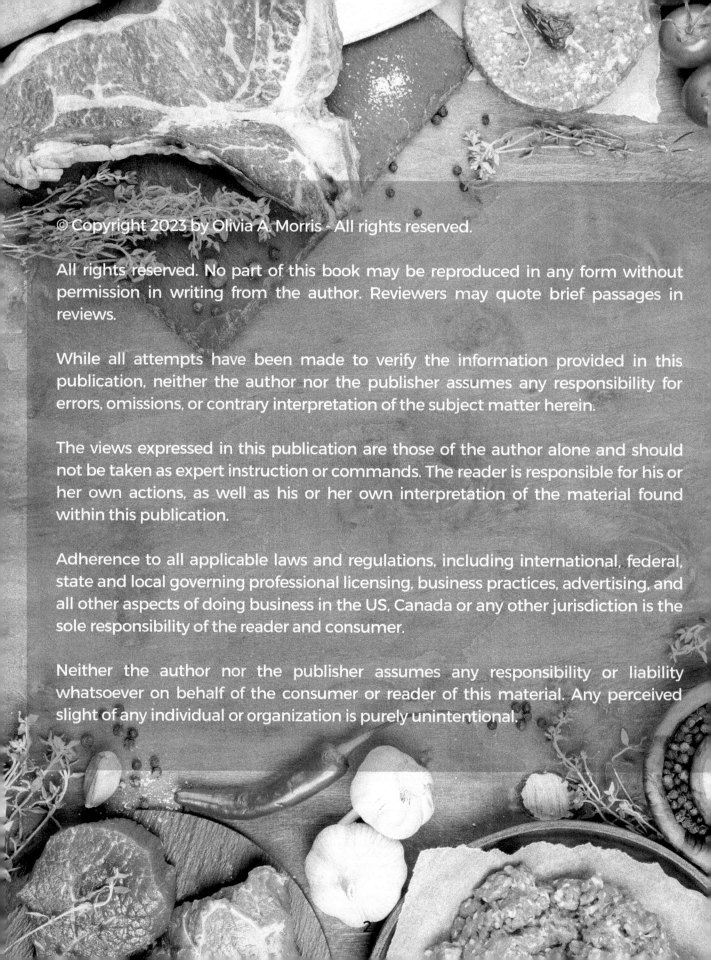

TABLE OF CONTENTS

INTRODUCTION

In this age of fast food and hectic lifestyles, it has become increasingly important to maintain a healthy diet and consume nutritious and delicious foods. Homemade canned meats are an excellent solution to this problem; they provide long-lasting, protein-rich alternatives to traditional supermarket meats while maintaining exceptional flavor and texture.

Throughout this book, we will delve into the process of meat canning, explaining step-by-step how to preserve your favorite cuts safely. We will also explore different cooking techniques for canned meats, ensuring you have all the tools to transform them into mouth-watering dishes.

The "**MEAT CANNING COOKBOOK**" is divided into chapters dedicated to a specific type of meat, poultry, or game. From the classics like beef, pork, and chicken to more adventurous options such as venison and rabbit – there is truly something for every palate. You'll be delighted by the myriad flavors that await you as you explore creative culinary combinations using various preservation techniques.

We have made every effort to ensure this book is informative and user-friendly. Packed with clear instructions and handy tips and tricks from experienced canning aficionados, this cookbook will be invaluable for seasoned home cooks and beginners who wish to try this rewarding and cost-effective food preservation method.

THE BENEFITS OF
HOMEMADE CANNED MEAT

Canning meat at home has become increasingly popular in recent years as more and more people realize the benefits of this ancient food preservation technique. Making homemade canned meat with the help of a pressure cooker is an eco-friendly and money-saving practice. It also ensures our pantry always has a delicious, healthy, and ready-to-eat meal option. This section will highlight the various advantages of canning your meat.

1. Improved Food Quality: You can choose high-quality cuts from your trusted sources by canning your meat at home. This control over the ingredients ensures that your food is healthy and fresh, ultimately leading to a better taste experience.

2. Cost Savings: Canning meat yourself can save you money compared to purchasing canned products from the supermarket. Your cost per can will usually be lower since you can take advantage of sales or invest in bulk purchases.

3. Reduced Preservatives: Store-bought canned products often contain excessive sodium and other preservatives to elongate their shelf life. With homemade canned meat, you have full control over the ingredients, thus maintaining the original nutritional value of the food.

4. Emergency Preparedness: Having a stable stock of varied homemade canned goods can be advantageous during emergencies or unforeseen circumstances when regular grocery shopping isn't possible.

HOW TO USE HOMEMADE CANNED MEATS IN RECIPES

Canning your meats at home is a great way to preserve the freshness and flavor of locally sourced or homegrown meats. In addition, it can save you money on groceries and reduce waste. But how do you incorporate these homemade canned meats into everyday meals? Here, we will provide tips and tricks for using canned meats in meal recipes that are both delicious and satisfying.

1. Start with Easy-To-Adapt Recipes: When starting with homemade canned meats, choose easy to adapt recipes to accommodate the canned ingredients. Consider your staple family recipes like spaghetti Bolognese, chili con carne, or pot pies – all you have to do is substitute the fresh meat in these dishes with the canned version.

2. Use Canned Meats for Quick Meals: Homemade canned meats can be a lifesaver when you want a quick meal after a long day at work. Toss some canned chicken into a stir-fry, add canned beef to a pasta sauce, or mix canned pulled pork into macaroni and cheese for an easy and delicious meal.

3. Incorporate Canned Meats into Salad: Hearty ethnic salads are perfect for incorporating canned meats. Think Greek salads with added canned chicken, taco salads featuring canned beef, or salad Niçoise enhanced with some canned tuna. Use your imagination when creating salads featuring homemade canned meats.

4. Make Hearty Sandwiches and Wraps: Canned meats make excellent sandwich fillings! Just drain off any excess liquid and mix the meat with your choice of additional ingredients - mayonnaise, mustard, veggies, relishes, or chutneys - to create a delicious and satisfying instant sandwich filling.

5. Explore Various Cuisine Types: The versatility of homemade canned meats allows you to experiment with cuisines worldwide. Mexican enchiladas, Italian pasta dishes, American BBQ-style pulled pork, and Indian curries can all be made easily using canned meats.

6. Make Meal Prep Easy with Casseroles: Meat-based casseroles are another way to use homemade canned meats. Simply replace the fresh meat in the recipe with the canned version and enjoy a warm and comforting meal. Beyond that, many casseroles freeze well to prepare multiple servings at once.

7. Plan and Be Creative: You can get the most out of your homemade canned meats by planning your meals and being creative with your recipe adaptations. Don't be afraid to swap out a component from a new recipe or add your twist.

PRESSURE CANNING VS. WATER BATH CANNING

Canning is a popular method of preserving food and extending its shelf life. Whether you're a beginner or a seasoned expert in home food preservation, understanding the differences between pressure canning and water bath canning is vital. This chapter will explore the benefits, drawbacks, and suitable applications of these two canning methods.

PRESSURE CANNING

Pressure canning is a preservation method that uses high temperatures to destroy bacteria, yeast, and other microorganisms that can spoil food. It involves heating the food in jars to a specific temperature using pressurized steam. This method reaches temperatures of 240°F (116°C) or higher, effectively killing harmful bacteria and making it safe for long-term storage.

BENEFITS OF PRESSURE CANNING
1. **Higher temperature** - Since pressure canning achieves a higher temperature than water bath canning, it kills potential contaminants in low-acid foods like vegetables and meats more effectively.
2. **Better for low-acid foods** - Pressure canning is recommended for low-acid foods such as meat, poultry, and most vegetables.
3. **Longer shelf life** - Generally offers a longer shelf life than water bath canning because of the sterile environment created during the process.

DRAWBACKS OF PRESSURE CANNING
1. **Specialized equipment** - Requires specialized equipment like a pressure canner.
2. **More complex** - The process is more complex than water bath canning due to the need for proper pressure control.
3. **Time-consuming** - Filling and sealing jars takes longer in this method.

WATER BATH CANNING

Water bath canning, also known as boiling water canning, is a different preservation method that relies on boiling water to heat the food jars. This process works best with acidic foods like fruits, jams, jellies, pickles, and some salsas, which have enough acidity to inhibit harmful bacteria growth. This method submerges jar-filled food in boiling water, achieving temperatures of 212°F (100°C).

BENEFITS OF WATER BATH CANNING
1. **Simpler process** - A simpler method than pressure canning, especially for beginners.
2. **Suitable for high-acid foods** - Ideal for preserving acidic foods such as fruits, pickles, and jams.
3. **Less expensive equipment** - Requires basic equipment like a large pot, making it more accessible.

DRAWBACKS OF WATER BATH CANNING

1. Limited to high-acid foods - Only suitable for high-acid foods due to their relatively lower temperature.

2. Not effective for low-acid foods – Not recommended for low-acid foods like non-pickled vegetables or meats, as it does not reach the necessary temperatures to kill harmful bacteria.

Both pressure canning and water bath canning have their unique benefits and drawbacks. To determine the best method for your preservation needs, consider the type of food you're preserving and its acidity level. Use pressure canning for low-acid foods like vegetables and meats and water bath canning for high-acid foods like fruits and pickles. By understanding these differences, you can make informed decisions about your home food preservation efforts and ensure the safety and quality of your canned goods.

BEFORE WE START PRESSURE CANNING

Before you dive headfirst into the world of pressure canning, it's essential to understand some basics. In this chapter, we'll discuss what you should know about your pressure canner, pressure canning methods, what foods can be canned, and what should not be canned.

KNOWING YOUR PRESSURE CANNER

Before you begin pressure canning, it's crucial to familiarize yourself with your pressure canner. A pressure canner is a specific type of heavy-duty pot that comes equipped with a tight-fitting lid and an adjustable pressure valve. There are two primary types of pressure canners: weighted gauge and dial gauge.
Weighted gauge canners use weight as the regulator, while dial gauge canners use a spinning dial. While both options are suitable for essential home-canning tasks, dial gauge models require annual calibration to ensure accuracy. Reading your user manual is also essential to know the specific features of your pressure canner and understand how to use it safely.

MEAT PRESSURE CANNING METHODS

In this section, we will be discussing step-by-step meat pressure canning methods for both beginners and experienced canners.
Equipment Needed:
- Pressure Canner
- Mason Jars with Lids and Bands
- Canning Tongs or Jar Lifter
- A Funnel
- A Ladle
- A Chopstick, Skewer, or Plastic Spatula (for removing air bubbles)
- A Clean Damp Cloth (to wipe the jar rims)

STEP-BY-STEP MEAT PRESSURE CANNING METHODS

Step 1: Choose Your Meat- Select fresh, high-quality meats for the best results when pressure canning. You can use any meat, such as beef, pork, chicken, turkey, fish, or even wild game.
Step 2: Prepare Your Meat- Cut your meat into uniform pieces to ensure even cooking during the canning process. Trim away excess fat, gristle, and bones.
Step 3: Prepare Your Jars- Wash and sterilize Mason jars by boiling them in water for 10 minutes or placing them on a dishwasher's sanitizing cycle.
Step 4: Packing Your Jars- There are two packing methods to choose from:
- Raw Pack Method – Place uncooked meat pieces directly into the jars, leaving 1-inch headspace.
- Hot Pack Method – Cook or brown meat in a skillet before packing them into jars, leaving 1-inch headspace.

Step 5: Add Liquid (Optional)- For the hot pack method, you can add hot meat broth, water, or tomato juice into the jar to cover the meat, leaving 1-inch headspace. The raw pack method doesn't require additional liquid.

Step 6: Remove Air Bubbles and Wipe Rims- Remove any air bubbles above using a chopstick or plastic spatula. Wipe the jar's rims with a clean, damp cloth to ensure secure lid placement.

Step 7: Attach Lids and Bands- Place sterilized lids on each jar and screw on bands until fingertip tight. Do not over-tighten.

Step 8: Place Jars in Pressure Canner- Use canning tongs or a jar lifter to lower your filled jars onto the canner rack. Arrange them so they're not touching one another or the sides of the canner.

Step 9: Process Your Jars- Refer to your pressure canner manufacturer's instructions for correct pressure levels and processing times according to specific meat types and jar sizes.

Step 10: Cool Your Jars- After processing is done, turn off the heat and allow pressure to return to zero. Wait for around 10-15 minutes, then remove jars using an oven mitt or thick towel. Place jars on a towel-covered surface away from drafts, allowing them to cool for approximately 24 hours.

Step 11: Check for Seal- Press the center of each jar lid; if it doesn't flex up or down, your seal is good. If it flexes or makes a popping noise, reprocesses or refrigerate that jar and use it within a few days.

Step 12: Label and Store Your Jars- Label jars with the content and date, then store them in a cool, dark, dry place. Pressure-canned meats typically have a shelf life of one to two years when properly stored.

By following this step-by-step meat pressure canning method, you can preserve your favorite cuts of meat safely and efficiently.

WHAT CAN BE CANNED

Pressure canning is ideal for low-acid foods and products with a pH level greater than 4.6. Some examples of low-acid foods suitable for pressure canning include:

- Meat and poultry
- Fish and seafood
- Vegetables like green beans, corn, peas, and potatoes
- Soups and stews
- Tomato products mixed with low-acid ingredients
- Chili and spaghetti sauce

The high heat and pressure required for these types of food destroy harmful bacteria, ensuring safe consumption when stored properly.

WHAT SHOULD NOT BE CANNED

Although pressure canning allows you to preserve a wide variety of foods, certain items should not be canned due to safety reasons or unsuitable texture after processing:

- Dairy products like butter, milk, soft cheese, or cream
- Highly-starchy foods
- Pureed vegetables like mashed pumpkin or other squash varieties
- Thick sauces that won't allow heat to circulate adequately during processing

It's crucial to adhere to tested recipes and guidelines recommended by

By understanding the basics discussed in this chapter, you'll be well-equipped to begin your pressure-canning journey confidently and safely. Remember always to follow approved recipes and guidelines to ensure the quality and safety of your preserved goods throughout the year.

BEEF

Classic Beef Stew

PREPARATION TIME
30 Minutes

COOKING TIME
75 Minutes

JAR SIZE
Quart Sized

YELD
4 to 5 Jars

PRESSURE
10 to 11 PSI

INGREDIENTS

- 3 pounds beef, cubed
- 3 cups potatoes, cubed
- 2 cups carrots, peeled and sliced
- 1 cup onions, chopped
- 2 cloves garlic, minced
- 4 cups beef broth
- 2 tbsp vegetable oil
- 1 tbsp Worcestershire sauce
- 1/4 cup flour
- Salt & pepper to taste

PROCEDURE

1. Heat vegetable oil in the pressure cooker over medium heat. Add beef cubes and cook until browned on all sides.

2. Stir in onions and garlic, then cook within 5 minutes. Add potatoes, carrots, salt, pepper, Worcestershire sauce, and mix well.

3. Sprinkle flour over and give a good stir until everything is coated. Pour the beef broth and stir well.

4. Lock your pressure cooker lid and cook on high pressure within 30 minutes.

5. Allow your pressure cooker to release its pressure naturally before carefully opening the lid.

6. Ladle hot stew into sterilized jars, leaving a 1" headspace at the top of each jar.

7. Wipe jar rims clean with a damp cloth and attach two-piece lids tightly.

8. Fill your pressure canner with water according to the manufacturer's instructions and load jars onto the canning rack.

9. Place the lid on the canner, make sure it is secure, and process at 11 psi (for weighted gauge canner) or 10 psi (for dial gauge canner) within 75 minutes.

10. Allow jars to cool completely for 12-24 hours before checking the seals, labeling them, and storing them in a cool, dark place.

Teriyaki-Glazed Sliced Sirloin Steak

PREPARATION TIME

30 Minutes

COOKING TIME

75 Minutes

JAR SIZE

Pint Sized

YELD

4 to 5 Jars

PRESSURE

11 PSI

INGREDIENTS

- 2 pounds sirloin steak, thinly
- sliced
- 1 cup teriyaki sauce
- 2 tbsp olive oil
- 1/2 cup soy sauce
- 1/4 cup brown sugar
- 2 garlic cloves, minced
- 1 tbsp ginger, grated
- 1 tbsp cornstarch
- 2 tbsp water

PROCEDURE

1. Combine teriyaki, soy sauce, brown sugar, garlic, and ginger in a bowl. Mix well until sugar is dissolved and set aside.

2. Heat olive oil in your skillet over medium heat. Add the sliced sirloin steak and cook until brown on both sides. Remove from heat.

3. In a separate small bowl, dissolve cornstarch in water and stir it into the teriyaki sauce mixture.

4. Pour the teriyaki sauce mixture over the cooked sirloin steak slices in the skillet, stirring to coat evenly.

5. Transfer the teriyaki-glazed sirloin steak slices into clean quart jars, leaving a 1" headspace at the top of each jar.

6. Wipe jar rims clean with a damp cloth and attach two-piece lids tightly.

7. Fill your pressure canner with water according to the manufacturer's instructions and load jars onto the canning rack.

8. Place the lid on the canner, make sure it is secure, and process at 11 psi within 75 minutes.

9. Allow jars to cool completely for 12-24 hours before checking the seals, labeling them, and storing them in a cool, dark place.

Spicy Chili With Meat

PREPARATION TIME
30 Minutes

COOKING TIME
95 Minutes

JAR SIZE
Pint Sized

YELD
6 Jars

PRESSURE
11 PSI

INGREDIENTS

- 3 pounds ground beef
- 2 large onions, chopped
- 4 cloves garlic, minced
- 2 (28 oz each) cans of crushed tomatoes
- 2 (15 oz each) cans of red kidney beans, drained & rinsed
- 1/4 cup chili powder
- 2 tsp ground cumin
- 1 tsp cayenne pepper
- Salt & pepper, to taste

PROCEDURE

1. In a pressure cooker, brown the ground beef and chopped onions until cooked through. Drain the grease.

2. Add the garlic and cook within 1 minute.

3. Add crushed tomatoes, pinto beans, red kidney beans, chili powder, ground cumin, cayenne pepper, salt, and pepper.

4. Lock the pressure cooker lid and set it to high pressure over high heat.

5. Cook the chili under high pressure for 20 minutes, then carefully release the pressure according to your cooker's instructions.

6. Prepare a water bath canner by filling it with water, placing the trivet or rack in the bottom of the pot, and heating the water to boiling.

7. Spoon hot chili into hot jars, leaving 1-inch headspace. Make sure to remove any air bubbles with a non-metallic spatula.

8. Wipe jar rims using a clean damp cloth and apply lids and bands until you reach fingertip tightness.

9. Place jars into boiling water using a jar lifter or tongs. Ensure that jars are covered by at least one inch of water.

10. Process pint jars at 11 psi (adjust for altitude) for 75 minutes and quart jars for 90 minutes.

11. Carefully remove jars from your canner and place them on a towel or cooling rack.

12. Allow jars to cool completely for 12-24 hours before checking the seals, labeling them, and storing them in a cool, dark place.

Mexican Shredded Beef Taco Filling

 PREPARATION TIME
30 Minutes

 COOKING TIME
2 Hours 45 Minutes

JAR SIZE
Pint Sized

 YELD
8 Jars

 PRESSURE
11 PSI

INGREDIENTS

- 4 pounds chuck roast, trimmed & cut into large chunks
- 2 tbsp vegetable oil
- 1 cup beef broth
- 1/2 cup apple cider vinegar
- 2 tbsp tomato paste
- 1 medium onion, chopped
- 4 cloves garlic, minced
- 2 tsp chili powder
- 1 tsp ground cumin
- 1 tsp dried oregano
- Salt & pepper to taste

PROCEDURE

1. In a pressure cooker, heat the vegetable oil over medium heat. Brown the beef chunks on all sides.

2. Add the onion and garlic with a pinch of salt and cook until they are softened.

3. Mix in the beef broth, apple cider vinegar, tomato paste, chili powder, ground cumin, and oregano. Stir well to combine.

4. Close the pressure cooker lid securely and cook on high pressure for 1 hour and 30 minutes.

5. Allow the pressure cooker to release naturally, then remove the beef from the liquid while reserving the liquid.

6. Shred the beef using two forks and mix it into the reserved liquid to keep it moist.

7. Prepare your clean, sterilized pint-sized mason jars with lids and bands.

8. Evenly distribute the shredded beef filling into the jars, leaving about 1" at the top for headspace.

9. Wipe the rims of each jar clean with a damp cloth, then place sterilized lids on top and secure them with bands.

10. Process jars in a pressure canner at 11 PSI (adjustments for altitude needed) for 75 minutes.

11. Allow jars to cool completely for 12-24 hours before checking the seals, labeling them, and storing them in a cool, dark place.

Porcupine Meatballs with Tomato Sauce

 PREPARATION TIME
30 Minutes

 COOKING TIME
2 Hours 45 Minutes

 JAR SIZE
Pint Sized

 YELD
4-5 Jars

PRESSURE
10 PSI

INGREDIENTS

- 2 pounds ground beef
- 1/2 cup uncooked white rice
- 1/2 cup water
- 1/4 cup chopped onions
- 1/4 cup chopped bell peppers
- 1 tsp salt
- 1 tsp black pepper
- 1 tsp garlic powder

Tangy Tomato Sauce:
- 3 cups tomato sauce
- 1/2 cup brown sugar
- 1/4 cup white vinegar
- 2 tbsp Worcestershire sauce

PROCEDURE

1. Combine ground beef, uncooked white rice, water, chopped onions, bell peppers, salt, black pepper, and garlic powder in a mixing bowl. Mix well.

2. Form the mixture into small meatballs of about 1-inch diameter.

3. Whisk together tomato sauce, brown sugar, white vinegar, and Worcestershire sauce in a separate mixing bowl to create the tangy tomato sauce.

4 .Place the meatballs in a pressure cooker and pour the tangy tomato sauce over them, ensuring they are completely covered.

5 .Close the pressure cooker lid, then cook on high pressure for 20 minutes.

6. After the pressure cooker cooking time is done, safely release the pressure and open the cooker.

7. Fill sterilized jars with meatballs and sauce, leaving 1" of headspace.

8 .Wipe rims clean with a damp cloth, then place the sterilized lids on jars and screw them tightly.

9. Process the jars in your pressure canner at 10 PSI within 75 minutes for pint jars.

Allow jars to cool completely for 12-24 hours before checking the seals, labeling them, and storing them in a cool, dark place.

Pot Roast with Vegetables

PREPARATION TIME

30 Minutes

COOKING TIME

90 Minutes

JAR SIZE

Quart Sized

YELD

4 Jars

PRESSURE

10-11 PSI

INGREDIENTS

- 4 pounds beef pot roast
- 2 pounds carrots, peeled & chopped
- 2 pounds potatoes, peeled & chopped
- 1-pound onions, chopped
- 3 cloves garlic, minced
- 1/4 cup vegetable oil
- Salt & pepper to taste
- 6 cups beef broth

PROCEDURE

1. Begin by preparing your pressure cooker canning setup according to the manufacturer's instructions.

2. In your large skillet, heat the vegetable oil over medium heat. Season the pot roast with salt plus pepper, then sear on all sides until browned. Remove from the skillet and set aside.

3. In the same skillet, sauté the onions and garlic for 5 minutes until softened.

4. Place the pot roast in the pressure cooker, followed by sautéed onions, garlic, carrots, potatoes, and beef broth.

5. Seal the pressure cooker according to its instructions and cook at 10-11 PSI for weighted-gauge cookers.

6. Reduce heat to maintain consistent pressure and cook for 90 minutes.

7. Carefully release pressure according to your cooker's instructions and transfer the pot roast with vegetables to sterilized jars using a slotted spoon, leaving about 1-inch headspace.

8. Ladle hot beef broth into each jar, maintaining a 1" headspace.

9. Wipe jar rims with a clean cloth or paper towel, secure lids, and process in a pressure cooker for canning according to your cooker's instructions.

10. Allow jars to cool completely for 12-24 hours before checking the seals, labeling them, and storing them in a cool, dark place.

Corned Beef and Cabbage

PREPARATION TIME	COOKING TIME	JAR SIZE	YELD	PRESSURE
30 Minutes	90 Minutes	Quart Sized	3-4 Jars	11 PSI

INGREDIENTS

- 4 pounds corned beef brisket, trimmed fat & cut into pieces
- 1 large head of cabbage, chopped into wedges
- 2 cups baby carrots
- 2 cups baby red potatoes, quartered
- 1 large onion, chopped
- 10 black peppercorns
- 5 cups water

PROCEDURE

1. Prepare your pressure cooker by setting a canning rack inside.

2. Place some corned beef, cabbage, carrots, potatoes, and onions in each sterilized jar, leaving a one-inch headspace.

3. Add one black peppercorn to each jar for flavor. Pour boiling water over the ingredients in each jar, maintaining a one-inch headspace.

4. Remove air bubbles from your jars using a non-metallic spatula. Adjust headspace if necessary.

5. Wipe the rims of your jars using a clean, damp cloth to remove any residue. Place the lids and rings on your jars and tighten them securely.

6. Load filled jars into the pressure cooker by following your cooker's manual for proper placement.

7. Close the pressure cooker's lid securely and set it to process at 11 PSI (adjust for altitude).

8. Allow the pressure cooker to vent steam for 10 minutes before applying the sealing weight/pressure regulator.

9. Process pint-sized jars within 75 minutes and quart-sized jars within 90 minutes at a specified pressure.

10 Once safe to access, use a jar lifter to remove jars from the pressure cooker and let them cool on your towel or cooling rack for 12-24 hours before checking the seals, labeling them, then storing them in a cool, dark place.

Tender Beef Bourguignon

PREPARATION TIME

30 Minutes

COOKING TIME

90 Minutes

JAR SIZE

Pint Sized

YELD

6 Jars

PRESSURE

11 PSI

INGREDIENTS

- 2 pounds beef chuck, cut into 1" cubes
- 4 slices bacon, chopped
- 1 (750ml) bottle of red wine
- 2 cups beef broth
- 1 onion, chopped
- 2 cloves garlic, minced
- 1 lb. button mushrooms, sliced
- 2 carrots, chopped
- 2 celery stalks, chopped
- 2 tbsp tomato paste
- 1 bay leaf
- Salt & pepper to taste

PROCEDURE

1. Over medium heat, cook bacon until brown and crisp in your large skillet. Remove from pan and set aside.

2. In the same skillet, brown beef in batches on all sides. Remove the beef and set aside.

3. Add onions, garlic, mushrooms, carrots, and celery to the skillet and cook within 5 minutes until slightly softened.

4. Add tomato paste to vegetables and cook for another minute. Return cooked bacon and beef to the skillet along with vegetables.

5. Pour red wine and broth into your skillet. Add bay leaf, salt, and pepper. Let it simmer.

6. Preheat your pressure canner according to the manufacturer's instructions.

7. Carefully ladle hot mixture into sterilized jars with a wide-mouth funnel, leaving a one-inch headspace.

8. Wipe rims using a clean damp cloth, place lids on jars, then tighten rings just enough.

9. Place jars into the pressure canner filled with water as specified by the manufacturer's instructions.

10. Close the pressure canner lid and increase heat to high, and set to process at 11 PSI. Process jars for 75 minutes, adjusting for altitude if necessary.

11. Turn off the heat, wait for the pressure to release completely, and carefully open the canner.

12. Once safe to access, use a jar lifter to remove jars from the pressure cooker and let them cool on your towel or cooling rack for 12-24 hours before checking the seals, labeling them, then storing them in a cool, dark place.

Ground Beef and Rice Stuffed Peppers

PREPARATION TIME

30 Minutes

COOKING TIME

75 Minutes

JAR SIZE

Quart Sized

YELD

6 Jars

PRESSURE

11 PSI

INGREDIENTS

- 6 large bell peppers, cut the tops, seeded & cored
- 1 pound ground beef
- 1 cup cooked rice
- 1 small onion, finely chopped
- 2 cloves garlic, minced
- 1 (15 oz) can of tomato sauce
- 1 tsp salt
- 1/2 tsp pepper
- 1/2 tsp oregano
- 1 cup shredded cheddar cheese

PROCEDURE

1. Combine ground beef, rice, onion, garlic, 1/2 can of tomato sauce, salt, pepper, paprika, and oregano in your large bowl.

2. Stuff each bell pepper with the ground beef and rice mixture. Pour your remaining tomato sauce on top of each stuffed pepper.

3. Place the stuffed peppers in a pressure canning jar with at least half an inch of headspace at the top.

4. Seal your jars with their lids and rings but do not tighten completely.

5. Place sealed jars on a pressure canner rack (leaving some space between each jar).

6. Close the lid securely and set the PRESSURE to 11 PSI. Cook at this pressure for 75 minutes.

7. After cooking is complete, let the canner cool down naturally before releasing any remaining steam.

8. Once safe to access, use a jar lifter to remove jars from the pressure cooker and let them cool on your towel or cooling rack for 12-24 hours before checking the seals, labeling them, then storing them in a cool, dark place.

Savory Shepherd's Pie in a Jar

PREPARATION TIME

30 Minutes

COOKING TIME

105 Minutes

JAR SIZE

Pint Sized

YELD

4 Jars

PRESSURE

10 PSI

INGREDIENTS

- 2 pounds ground beef
- 1 large onion, chopped
- 2 carrots, chopped
- 1 cup frozen peas
- 1 cup frozen corn
- 2 cloves garlic, minced
- 2 tbsp tomato paste
- 1/2 cup beef broth
- 1 tbsp Worcestershire sauce
- Salt & pepper, to taste
- 4 cups mashed potatoes

PROCEDURE

1. In your large skillet, brown the beef over medium heat, seasoning with salt plus pepper. Remove and set aside.

2. In your same skillet, cook the onion and carrots for 5 minutes until softened. Add the frozen peas and corn, cooking within 5 minutes until heated through.

3. Stir in the garlic, tomato paste, beef broth, and Worcestershire sauce. Cook within 5 minutes until everything is well combined.

4. Preheat your pressure canner to 10 PSI.

5. Assemble your jars by adding a layer of the cooked meat mixture to each jar, followed by a layer of mashed potatoes on top, leaving 1" of headspace at the top.

6. Wipe the rims clean and place lids and bands onto the jars. Place jars in a pressure canner according to the manufacturer's instructions.

7. Process at recommended PRESSURE (10 PSI) for 90 minutes once full steam has been reached.

8. Remove and let the canner cool naturally before carefully removing jars with a jar lifter and placing them onto a towel-lined surface.

9. Let the jars cool and check for proper seals. Any jars that haven't been sealed properly should be refrigerated and consumed within a few days.

Juicy Sloppy Joes

PREPARATION TIME

30 Minutes

COOKING TIME

80 Minutes

JAR SIZE

Pint Sized

YELD

4 Jars

PRESSURE

10 PSI

INGREDIENTS

- 2 pounds ground beef
- 1 large onion, chopped
- 1 green bell pepper, chopped
- 3 cloves garlic, minced
- 1 cup ketchup
- 1/4 cup brown sugar
- 2 tbsp Worcestershire sauce
- 1 tbsp prepared mustard
- Salt & pepper to taste

PROCEDURE

1. Cook ground beef in your large skillet over medium heat until it's no longer pink.

2. Add the onion, green pepper, plus garlic to the skillet and cook until the vegetables soften.

3. Stir in ketchup, brown sugar, Worcestershire, mustard, salt, and pepper. Simmer within 5 minutes.

4. Transfer the cooked mixture to sterilized canning jars, leaving 1-inch headspace.

5. Wipe the jar rims clean and center the lids on top; screw on the bands until fingertip-tight.

6. Place filled jars in a pressure canner with sufficient water to cover halfway up the jars. Process the jars at 10 PSI within 75 minutes (adjust for altitudeOnce safe to access, use a jar lifter to remove jars from the pressure cooker and let them cool on your towel or cooling rack for 12-24 hours before checking the seals, labeling them, then storing them in a cool, dark place.

Hearty Beef Goulash

PREPARATION TIME

30 Minutes

COOKING TIME

2 Hours 40 Minutes

JAR SIZE

Pint Sized

YELD

4 Jars

PRESSURE

10-11 PSI

INGREDIENTS

- 2 pounds beef stew meat, sliced into 1" cubes
- 2 medium onions, chopped
- 2 cloves garlic, minced
- 1 green bell pepper, chopped
- 1 red bell pepper, chopped
- 3 cups diced tomatoes with juice
- 1 cup beef broth
- 2 tbsp tomato paste
- 2 tbsp paprika
- 1 tbsp olive oil
- Salt & pepper to taste

PROCEDURE

1. In your large skillet, heat the olive oil over medium-high heat. Add the beef, then cook until browned. Remove and set aside.

2. In the same skillet, add onions, garlic, and bell peppers. Cook within 3 minutes until softened.

3. Stir in your diced tomatoes with their juice, beef broth, tomato paste, paprika, salt, and pepper. Let it boil.

4. Adjust to a simmer and add the beef cubes. Cook within an hour until the beef is tender.

5. Fill hot goulash into sterilized jars, leaving 1-inch headspace. Remove air bubbles using a non-metallic spatula and adjust the headspace if needed.

6. Wipe jar rims with a clean cloth or paper towel soaked in vinegar to ensure no food particles remain. Secure lids and rings on the jars.

7. Place jars in a pressure canner and process at 11 PSI (for weighted-gauge canners) or 10 PSI (for dial-gauge canners). Adjust pressure for higher altitudes if necessary.

8. Process pint jars within 75 minutes and quart jars within 90 minutes. Turn off the heat and let the pressure to drop naturally before removing the lid.

9. Carefully remove jars from the canner using a jar lifter and let them cool on your towel or wire rack.

Easy Beef Stroganoff

PREPARATION TIME	COOKING TIME	JAR SIZE	YELD	PRESSURE
30 Minutes	40 Minutes	Pint Sized	4-6 Jars	11 PSI

INGREDIENTS

- 2 pounds beef sirloin, cut into thin strips
- 1 large onion, finely chopped
- 3 cups fresh mushrooms, sliced
- 2 cloves garlic, minced
- 2 tbsp vegetable oil
- 1 cup beef broth
- 1 cup sour cream
- 1 (10.5 oz) can of condensed cream of mushroom soup
- Salt & pepper, to taste

PROCEDURE

`1. Prepare a pressure cooker by placing a rack or trivet at the bottom.

2. Heat vegetable oil in your skillet over medium-high heat. Add beef strips and cook until browned. Remove and place into a large mixing bowl.

3. In the same skillet, cook onion, garlic, and mushrooms until the onion is translucent and the mushrooms are softened. Add to the mixing bowl with beef.

4. Mix beef broth, sour cream, and cream of mushroom soup until well combined.

5. Pour this sauce over the beef mixture and stir well to coat evenly. Add salt and pepper to taste.

6. Spoon the stroganoff mixture carefully into clean sterilized jars, leaving about 1-inch headspace from the top of the jar.

7. Wipe jar rims clean of any residue with a damp cloth or paper towel.

8. Place canning lids securely onto jars and tighten screw bands until fingertip-tight.

9. Carefully lower filled jars into the pressure cooker on top of the rack or trivet.

10. Follow your pressure cooker's instructions for canning, setting it to 11 PSI for weighted gauge or dial-gauge cookers.

11. Process jars within 20 minutes, adjusting for altitude as needed.

12. Carefully remove hot jars using a jar lifter and place them on your cooling rack or towel-lined countertop.

13. Allow jars to cool completely and check seals before storing.

Swiss Steak with Tomato Gravy

PREPARATION TIME

30 Minutes

COOKING TIME

90 Minutes

JAR SIZE

Pint Sized

YELD

6 Jars

PRESSURE

11 PSI

INGREDIENTS

- 3 pounds Swiss steak, cut into serving-sized pieces
- 1/2 cup all-purpose flour
- 1/4 cup vegetable oil
- 2 onions, thinly sliced
- 1 red bell pepper, sliced
- 2 carrots, sliced
- 2 garlic cloves, minced
- 1 (28 oz) can of crushed tomatoes
- 1 tbsp Worcestershire sauce
- Salt & pepper to taste

PROCEDURE

1. Season the steak pieces with salt plus pepper, then coat with flour.

2. In your pressure, cooker over medium heat, add the vegetable oil and brown the steak on both sides. Remove.

3. Add onions, bell pepper, carrots, and garlic to the pressure cooker and cook within a few minutes until softened.

4. Put the steak back into the pressure cooker and add crushed tomatoes and Worcestershire sauce.

5. Close the pressure cooker lid securely and set the cooker to high pressure. Cook within 90 minutes.

6. Once done cooking, let the pressure release naturally. Fill sterilized canning jars with hot Swiss steak mixture, leaving 1-inch headspace.

7. Wipe jar rims clean, place lids on jars, and screw bands until finger tight.

8. Process filled pint jars using a pressure canner at 11 PSI for 75 minutes.

9. Carefully remove hot jars using a jar lifter and place them on your cooling rack or towel-lined countertop.

10. Allow jars to cool completely and check seals before storing.

Beef in Wine Sauce

PREPARATION TIME
30 Minutes

COOKING TIME
75 Minutes

JAR SIZE
Quart Sized

YELD
4 Jars

PRESSURE
11 PSI

INGREDIENTS

- 4 pounds beef chuck roast, cut into 1-inch cubes
- 2 cups red wine
- 2 medium onions, chopped
- 3 cloves garlic, minced
- 1 cup beef broth
- 1 tbsp Worcestershire sauce
- 2 tbsp tomato paste
- 2 tsp dried thyme
- Salt & pepper to taste
- 2 tbsp vegetable oil

PROCEDURE

1. Heat the vegetable oil in a pressure cooker over medium-high heat. Add the beef cubes, then brown on all sides. Remove and set aside.

2. In the same pressure cooker, add onions and garlic, and sauté until they are softened.

3. Add the beef back into the pressure cooker with onions and garlic.

4. Stir in the red wine, broth, Worcestershire, tomato paste, thyme, salt, and pepper. Let it simmer.

5. Close the pressure cooker lid securely and cook on high pressure for 15 minutes.

6. After the cooking time is finished, release the pressure according to your pressure cooker's instruction manual.

7. Transfer the hot Beef in Wine Sauce mixture into hot sterilized jars, leaving a 1-inch headspace at the top of each jar.

8. Wipe the rims of your jars using a damp cloth and secure them with canning lids and rings.

9. Place jars in a pressure canner filled with water according to your canner's instructions.

10. Set at 11 PSI, and adjust accordingly for higher altitudes. Process the jars within 75 minutes.

11. Carefully remove hot jars using a jar lifter and place them on your cooling rack or towel-lined countertop.

12. Allow jars to cool completely and check seals before storing.

Mongolian Beef Stir-Fry

PREPARATION TIME

30 Minutes

COOKING TIME

75 Minutes

JAR SIZE

Pint Sized

YELD

6-8 Jars

PRESSURE

11 PSI

INGREDIENTS

- 2 pounds beef flank, thinly sliced
- 1/2 cup soy sauce
- 1/4 cup brown sugar
- 3 cloves garlic, minced
- 1 tbsp fresh ginger, minced
- 2 tbsp cornstarch
- 3 green onions, chopped
- 1/4 cup vegetable oil
- 1 red bell pepper, sliced
- 1 cup snow peas
- 2 cups water

PROCEDURE

1. Combine the soy sauce, sugar, garlic, and ginger in your medium bowl. Add the beef and let marinate for 15 minutes.

2. Drain the beef from your marinade and reserve the liquid. Toss the beef with cornstarch to coat evenly.

3. Heat vegetable oil in your large skillet over high heat. Cook the beef until browned but not fully cooked. Set aside.

4. Add more oil if needed in the same skillet and stir-fry red bell pepper and snow peas within 2 minutes.

5. Add the cooked beef back to the skillet with the reserved marinade and water. Let it simmer, then remove.

6. Pack hot stir-fry mixture into clean and sterilized pint jars, leaving a one-inch headspace in each jar.

7. Wipe jar rims clean and apply lids and bands securely but not too tight. Process at 10 PSI (adjust altitude as needed) for 75 minutes.

8. Allow the pressure canner to cool naturally before removing the weighted gauge or vent lock.

9. Wait 10 minutes before removing jars from your canner.

Asian-Style Soy Sesame Beef

PREPARATION TIME
30 Minutes

COOKING TIME
75 Minutes

JAR SIZE
Pint Sized

YELD
6-8 Jars

PRESSURE
11 PSI

INGREDIENTS

- 3 pounds lean beef, cut into 1-inch cubes
- 1 cup soy sauce
- 1/4 cup sesame oil
- 1/4 cup packed brown sugar
- 2 tbsp minced garlic
- 2 tbsp grated fresh ginger
- 2 tbsp rice vinegar
- 1 tbsp red pepper flakes (optional)
- 1 cup thinly sliced green onions
- 1/4 cup toasted sesame seeds
- Salt & pepper to taste

PROCEDURE

1. Combine soy sauce, sesame oil, brown sugar, garlic, ginger, rice vinegar, and red pepper flakes in a large bowl.

2. Add the beef cubes, ensuring that all pieces are fully covered. Cover the bowl and refrigerate within 20 minutes or overnight for better flavor.

3. Heat a large skillet over medium-high heat. Sear the marinated beef on all sides until browned.

4. Pack the seared beef into clean and sterilized jars, making sure to leave at least a one-inch headspace. Pour the remaining marinade on top of each jar evenly.

5. Sprinkle green onions and toasted sesame seeds over each jar's contents.

6. Wipe the jar rims clean with a damp cloth, place lids on jars, and then secure them with bands following proper canning procedures.

7. Load jars into a pressure canner following manufacturers' guidelines and process at a PRESSURE of 11 PSI for 75 minutes.

8. Turn off the heat, then let the pressure release naturally. Wait until the pressure is entirely released before removing the jars.

9. Remove jars from the canner, let cool, and check seals before storing.

Italian Beef Ragù

PREPARATION TIME
30 Minutes

COOKING TIME
120 Minutes

JAR SIZE
Pint Sized

YELD
8 Jars

PRESSURE
11 PSI

INGREDIENTS

- 2 pounds beef chuck, cut into 1-inch cubes
- 3 tbsp olive oil
- 1 large onion, chopped
- 2 carrots, chopped
- 2 celery stalks, chopped
- 4 cloves garlic, minced
- 1 cup red wine (optional)
- 1 (28 oz) can crushed tomatoes in tomato puree or juice
- 1 tbsp tomato paste
- 1 tsp salt
- 1/2 tsp black pepper
- 1 tsp dried oregano or Italian seasoning

PROCEDURE

1. Heat the olive oil in your large skillet over medium heat. Brown the beef cubes on all sides. Set aside.

2. Add the chopped onion, carrots, celery, and garlic to your skillet. Cook within 5 minutes until they soften.

3. Stir in the browned beef cubes and cook within two minutes.

4. Add the red wine (if using) to deglaze the pan. Let it simmer and cook until reduced by half.

5. Add crushed tomatoes, tomato paste, salt, pepper, and oregano/Italian seasoning to the pan.

6. Let it boil over high heat and adjust to low heat; cover and cook within 1 hour, stirring occasionally.

7. Pack the Italian beef ragu into clean and sterilized jars, leaving at least a one-inch headspace.

8. Wipe the jar rims clean with a damp cloth, place lids on jars, and then secure them with bands following proper canning procedures.

9. Start heating your pressure canner slowly, aiming for a pressure of 11 PSI. Once it reaches the required pressure, process the jars for 90 minutes.

10. Turn off the heat, let the pressure drop naturally, and allow the canner to cool down completely before removing the jars carefully.

11. Place the sealed jars on a kitchen towel and leave them undisturbed within 12 hours or overnight to cool and seal completely. Check the seals after 12 hours and store them properly.

POULTRY

Spiced Chicken & Vegetable Medley

PREPARATION TIME

30 Minutes

COOKING TIME

100 Minutes

JAR SIZE

Quart Sized

YELD

6 Jars

PRESSURE

11 PSI

INGREDIENTS

- 4 pounds boneless, skinless chicken breasts, cubed
- 2 cups chopped carrots
- 2 cups chopped bell peppers
- 2 cups chopped zucchini
- 1 cup chopped onions
- 3 cloves garlic, minced
- 1/4 cup olive oil
- 1/4 cup apple cider vinegar
- 1/2 cup water
- 2 tsp paprika
- 2 tsp ground cumin
- 1 tsp ground coriander
- Salt & pepper, to taste

PROCEDURE

1. Heat olive oil in your large skillet over medium-high heat. Add chicken and cook until lightly browned.

2. Add onions and garlic, then cook until they become soft and fragrant.

3. Mix in the remaining vegetables, apple cider vinegar, and water, stirring well.

4. Season with paprika, cumin, coriander, salt, and pepper. Cook within 5 minutes before removing from heat.

5. Fill quart-sized canning jars with the cooked chicken and vegetable mixture, leaving 1-inch headspace.

6. Wipe the rims of your jars and secure lids with bands, screwing them down finger tight.

7. Place jars on a pressure canner rack within the pressure canning pot.

8. Secure the lid of your pressure canner, set it to reach a PRESSURE of 11 PSI, and process it within 75 minutes.

9. After elapsed processing time, turn off the heat, let the canner cool, and depressurize completely before removing the lid.

10. Carefully remove jars and let them cool on a wire rack for 12-24 hours. Check lids for proper seals before storing.

Ginger-Soy Chicken Thighs

PREPARATION TIME
20 Minutes

COOKING TIME
75 Minutes

JAR SIZE
Pint Sized

YELD
6 Jars

PRESSURE
11 PSI

INGREDIENTS

- 4 pounds chicken thighs, boneless and skinless
- 1/4 cup soy sauce
- 1/4 cup honey
- 2 tbsp fresh ginger, grated
- 2 cloves garlic, minced
- 1 tsp sesame oil
- 1/4 tsp crushed red pepper flakes
- Salt & pepper, to taste

PROCEDURE

1. Mix the soy sauce, honey, ginger, garlic, sesame oil, and crushed red pepper flakes in your large bowl. Set aside.

2. Season the chicken thighs using salt and pepper. Add it to the marinade mixture and let it sit for at least 15 minutes.

3. Once marinated, pack the chicken thighs evenly into sterile pint-sized jars.

4. Divide the remaining marinade equally among the jars to cover the chicken.

5. Wipe rims and place lids onto jars with rings tightened finger tight. Place jars in a pressure canner filled with 2-4 inches of water.

6. Process at 11 psi for weighted-gauge or 10 psi for dial-gauge pressure canners for 75 minutes if using pint-sized jars.

7. After elapsed processing time, turn off the heat, let the canner cool, and depressurize completely before removing the lid.

8. Carefully remove jars and let them cool on a wire rack for 12-24 hours. Check lids for proper seals before storing.

Chicken Corn Chowder

PREPARATION TIME

30 Minutes

COOKING TIME

120 Minutes

JAR SIZE

Quart Sized

YELD

4 Jars

PRESSURE

11 PSI

INGREDIENTS

- 4 cups cooked, shredded chicken
- 4 cups fresh or frozen corn kernels
- 2 cups diced potatoes
- 1 cup chopped celery
- 1 cup chopped onion

- 2 cloves garlic, minced
- 4 cups chicken broth
- 2 cups heavy cream
- 2 tbsp butter
- Salt & pepper to taste

PROCEDURE

1. In your large pot, melt the butter over medium heat. Add the onion, celery, and garlic, then sauté within 5 minutes until the vegetables are tender.

2. Add the potatoes, chicken, corn, and broth. Let it boil, then reduce the heat and simmer within 20 minutes or until the potatoes are cooked through.

3. Add the heavy cream to your pot and season with salt and pepper. Stir well and simmer for another couple of minutes.

4. Ladle the hot chowder into sterilized jars, leaving a 1-inch headspace; remove any air bubbles with a non-metallic spatula.

5. Wipe jar rims with a clean cloth, place lids on jars, then secure them with jar bands; do not overtighten.

6. Place filled jars into a pressure canner and process at 11 PSI for 90 minutes.

7. After elapsed processing time, turn off the heat, let the canner cool, and depressurize completely before removing the lid.

8. Carefully remove jars and let them cool on a wire rack for 12-24 hours. Check lids for proper seals before storing.

BBQ Pulled Chicken

PREPARATION TIME

30 Minutes

COOKING TIME

45 Minutes

JAR SIZE

Quart Sized

YELD

6-7 Jars

PRESSURE

11 PSI

INGREDIENTS

- 4 pounds boneless, skinless chicken breasts
- 2 cups barbecue sauce
- 1/4 cup brown sugar
- 2 tbsp apple cider vinegar
- 1/2 tsp onion powder
- 1/2 tsp garlic powder
- Salt & pepper to taste

PROCEDURE

1. Place the chicken breasts on your cutting board and cut them into bite-sized chunks.

2. Combine the barbecue sauce, brown sugar, apple cider, Worcestershire sauce, onion powder, garlic powder, salt, and pepper in a large bowl.

3. Add the chicken chunks and toss until evenly coated.

4. Divide the pulled chicken mixture equally among well-cleaned and sterilized quart-size pressure canning jars.

5. With a damp cloth or paper towel, wipe off any barbecue sauce from the rims of your jars.

6. Lock down your pressure canner lid, adjust the cooking pressure to 11 PSI, and process within 45 minutes.

7. After elapsed processing time, turn off the heat, let the canner cool, and depressurize completely before removing the lid.

8. Carefully remove jars and let them cool on a wire rack for 12-24 hours. Check lids for proper seals before storing.

Spicy Chipotle Chicken Taco Filling

PREPARATION TIME
30 Minutes

COOKING TIME
105 Minutes

JAR SIZE
Pint Sized

YELD
8 Jars

PRESSURE
11 PSI

INGREDIENTS

- 4 pounds chicken breasts or thighs, boneless & skinless, trimmed excess fat & cut into small pieces
- 2 cups chopped onions
- 3 cloves garlic, minced
- 2 (14.5 oz) cans of diced tomatoes
- 1 cup chipotle peppers in
- adobo sauce, chopped
- 2 tsp ground cumin
- 1 tsp salt
- 1/2 tsp black pepper

PROCEDURE

1. In a large skillet, cook onions and garlic over medium heat for 5 minutes until they become soft and translucent.

2. Add the chicken and cook within 10 minutes until no longer pink.

3. Stir in the tomatoes, chipotle peppers, cumin, salt, and black pepper. Cook within 15 minutes.

4. Ladle the hot taco filling into sterilized jars, leaving 1-inch headspace. Wipe jar rims with a clean and damp cloth to ensure a proper seal.

5. Place lids on your jars and screw on bands until finger-tight—process jars in a pressure canner at 11 PSI for 75 minutes.

6. After elapsed processing time, turn off the heat, let the canner cool, and depressurize completely before removing the lid.

7. Carefully remove jars and let them cool on a wire rack for 12-24 hours. Check lids for proper seals before storing.

White Chicken Chili

PREPARATION TIME	COOKING TIME	JAR SIZE	YELD	PRESSURE
30 Minutes	100 Minutes	Pint Sized	8 Jars	11 PSI

INGREDIENTS

- 4 cups cooked white beans (cannellini or Great Northern)
- 2 pounds boneless, skinless chicken breasts, cooked and
- shredded
- 2 tbsp vegetable oil
- 1 large onion, diced
- 2 (4 oz each) cans of diced green chiles
- 1 tsp ground cumin
- 1 tsp dried oregano
- Salt & pepper to taste
- 4 cups chicken broth

PROCEDURE

1. In your large skillet, heat the vegetable oil over medium heat. Add the diced onion and cook within 5 minutes until translucent.

2. Add the garlic, green chiles, cumin, oregano, salt, and pepper. Cook within 3 minutes.

3. Combine the cooked white beans, chicken, and veggie-spice mixture in your large pressure canning pot. Pour the chicken broth and mix well.

4. Fill sterilized jars with the white chicken chili mixture up to 1" from the top.

5. Wipe the rims of your jars clean using a damp cloth, then secure the lids and rings tightly.

6. Place jars on the rack in your pressure canner using jar lifter tongs.

7. Lock your pressure canner lid securely, set it to 11 PSI, and cook for 90 minutes.

8. After elapsed processing time, turn off the heat and allow the canner to cool and depressurize completely before removing the lid.

9. Carefully remove jars and let them cool on a wire rack for 12-24 hours. Check lids for proper seals before storing.

Asian Chicken Thighs

PREPARATION TIME
25 Min + Marinating time

COOKING TIME
80 Minutes

JAR SIZE
Pint Sized

YELD
4 Jars

PRESSURE
11 PSI

INGREDIENTS

- 3 pounds boneless, skinless chicken thighs
- 1/2 cup soy sauce
- 1/4 cup rice vinegar
- 1/4 cup honey
- 2 tbsp sesame oil

- 1 tbsp minced garlic
- 1 tbsp minced ginger
- 1 tbsp cornstarch
- 2 green onions, chopped

PROCEDURE

1. Combine soy sauce, rice vinegar, honey, sesame oil, garlic, and ginger in a bowl to create the marinade.

2. Place chicken thighs into your large ziplock bag and pour the marinade over them. Seal and refrigerate within an hour.

3. Preheat your pressure canner by adding water according to the manufacturer's instructions and turning the heat to medium-high.

4. Remove marinated chicken from the refrigerator and drain off the excess marinade.

5. In a hot skillet, briefly sear chicken thighs on a high heat within 2 minutes on each side until they get a nice caramelized crust.

6. Fill sterilized jars with seared chicken thighs, leaving an inch of headspace.

7. Boil the leftover marinade in a small saucepan. Gradually stir in cornstarch dissolved in cold water until thickened.

8. Pour the heated sauce over the chicken thighs, ensuring an inch of headspace.

9. Wipe jar rims with a clean cloth to ensure ideal sealing surfaces. Place lids and screw bands on jars finger-tight.

10. Place jars in the pressure canner according to the manufacturer's specifications.

11. Increase heat and let it boil. Vent steam within 10 minutes and then close the vent. Process chicken thighs at 11 PSI for 75 minutes for pint jars.

12. After elapsed processing time, turn off the heat, let the canner cool, and depressurize completely before removing the lid.

13. Carefully remove jars and let them cool on a wire rack for 12-24 hours. Check lids for proper seals before storing.

Pesto-Stuffed Chicken Thighs with Olives

PREPARATION TIME
30 Minutes

COOKING TIME
75 Minutes

JAR SIZE
Pint Sized

YELD
4 Jars

PRESSURE
11 PSI

INGREDIENTS

- 8 boneless, skinless chicken thighs
- 1 cup prepared pesto sauce
- 1 cup pitted Kalamata olives
- 2 cups chicken broth
- Salt & pepper to taste

PROCEDURE

1. Lay the chicken thighs out on a clean surface and season both sides using salt and pepper. Spread 2 tbsp pesto sauce onto each chicken thigh.

2. Evenly distribute the olives among the chicken thighs, placing them on the pesto.

3. Roll up the chicken thighs tightly and secure them with cooking twine.

4. Add the broth to a large pressure canner and place a canning rack at the bottom.

5. Carefully place the stuffed chicken thighs in the canning jars, ensuring they are packed tightly but do not become deformed.

6. Wipe the rims of your jars with a clean cloth and secure lids and bands onto the jars.

7. Place the jars in the pressure canner, ensuring they remain upright on the canning rack.

8. Lock the pressure cooker lid and heat over medium-high heat until steam begins to escape through the vent pipe.

9. Once steady steam is produced, allow it to vent within 10 minutes before placing the weight on to seal.

10. Bring to a pressure of 11 PSI for weighted gauge or dial gauge canners and process within 75 minutes (do not fluctuate).

11. After elapsed processing time, turn off the heat, let the canner cool, and depressurize completely before removing the lid.

12. Carefully remove jars and let them cool on a wire rack for 12-24 hours. Check lids for proper seals before storing.

Salsa Verde Chicken

PREPARATION TIME
30 Minutes

COOKING TIME
75 Minutes

JAR SIZE
Pint Sized

YELD
8-9 Jars

PRESSURE
11 PSI

INGREDIENTS

- 4 pounds chicken breasts or thighs, boneless & skinless, trimmed any excess fat & cut them into bite-sized pieces
- 3 cups store-bought salsa verde
- ½ cup chicken broth
- 1 onion, chopped
- 1 cup fresh cilantro, chopped
- 2 cloves garlic, minced
- Salt & black pepper, to taste

PROCEDURE

1. Combine salsa verde, chicken broth, chopped onion, cilantro, and minced garlic in a large bowl.

2. Add the chicken pieces, then mix until coated. Let the mixture sit within 10 minutes for the flavors to blend.

3. In a pressure canner, start heating water according to your equipment's instructions.

4. Fill each sterilized jar with the chicken mixture up to an inch below the rim, ensuring equal proportions of chicken and sauce in each jar.

5. Wipe off the rims of your jars using a clean cloth and tightly secure lids onto the jars.

6. Place jars in your pressure canner using a jar lifter or tongs.

7. Lock the pressure canner lid and heat it until you reach a PRESSURE of 11 PSI; adjust accordingly for higher elevations.

8. Process for 75 minutes, adjusting heat as needed to maintain steady pressure.

9. After elapsed processing time, turn off the heat, let the canner cool, and depressurize completely before removing the lid.

10. Carefully remove jars and let them cool on a wire rack for 12-24 hours. Check lids for proper seals before storing.

Sweet and Sour Chicken

PREPARATION TIME

20 Minutes

COOKING TIME

75 Minutes

JAR SIZE

Pint Sized

YELD

5 Jars

PRESSURE

11 PSI

INGREDIENTS

- 2 pounds of chicken breasts, boneless & skinless, cut into bite-sized pieces
- 1 cup pineapple chunks, drained
- 1 large green bell pepper, chopped
- 1 large red bell pepper, chopped
- 1 medium onion, chopped
- 1 cup ketchup
- ¼ cup soy sauce
- ¾ cup brown sugar
- ¾ cup water
- 2 cloves minced garlic
- ¾ cup white vinegar
- Salt & pepper to taste

PROCEDURE

1. Combine ketchup, soy sauce, white vinegar, water, brown sugar and minced garlic in your large bowl.

2. In a separate bowl, season chicken with salt and pepper.

3. Add it to the sauce mixture and coat evenly. Set aside within 15 minutes for marinating.

4. Evenly distribute the marinated chicken mixture among sterilized jars. Fill jars with the sauce mixture while leaving 1-inch headspace.

5. Wipe jar rims clean, then place lids and bands on the jars securely but not overly tight.

6. Place the jars in the pressure canner following the canner's instructions for layering and spacing.

7. Process jars in the pressure canner at 11 PSI for 75 minutes.

8. After elapsed processing time, turn off the heat, let the canner cool, and depressurize completely before removing the lid.

9. Carefully remove jars and let them cool on a wire rack for 12-24 hours. Check lids for proper seals before storing.

Chicken Cacciatore

PREPARATION TIME	COOKING TIME	JAR SIZE	YELD	PRESSURE
30 Minutes	2 Hours 10 Minutes	Pint Sized	6-8 Jars	11 PSI

INGREDIENTS

- 4 pounds boneless, skinless chicken thighs
- 2 cups diced tomatoes
- 1 cup sliced bell peppers
- 1 cup sliced onions
- 1 cup sliced mushrooms
- 3 cloves garlic, minced
- ½ cup red wine
- ¼ cup olive oil
- 2 tbsp chopped fresh basil
- 2 tbsp chopped fresh parsley
- 1 tsp dried oregano
- Salt & pepper, to taste

PROCEDURE

1. Heat the olive oil in your large skillet over medium heat. Add the chicken thighs and cook within 10 minutes until browned on all sides. Remove the chicken and set aside.

2. Add the onions, bell peppers, and garlic to your skillet—Sauté within 5 minutes until softened.

3. Add the mushrooms and cook within 5 minutes until they release their moisture. Stir in the tomatoes, red wine, basil, parsley, oregano, salt, and pepper.

4. Return the chicken to your pan and let it boil. Adjust to low heat and simmer within 30 minutes until cooked through.

5. Remove the chicken and shred it into smaller pieces. Fill clean jars with the shredded chicken, leaving about 1" headspace.

6. Ladle sauce over the chicken, leaving ½" headspace in each jar.

7. Wipe the rims of jars with a clean cloth and place lids and rings on jars according to the manufacturer's instructions.

8. Process jars in the pressure canner at 11 PSI for 75 minutes.

9. After elapsed processing time, turn off the heat, let the canner cool, and depressurize completely before removing the lid.

10. Carefully remove jars and let them cool on a wire rack for 12-24 hours. Check lids for proper seals before storing.

Dilled Turkey Pot Pie Filling

PREPARATION TIME
30 Minutes

COOKING TIME
90 Minutes

JAR SIZE
Quart Sized

YELD
6 Jars

PRESSURE
11 PSI

INGREDIENTS

- 4 cups diced cooked turkey
- 1 cup diced carrots
- 1 cup diced celery
- 1 cup diced onions
- 1 cup diced potatoes
- 1/2 cup chopped fresh dill
- 4 cups turkey broth
- 2 cups heavy cream
- Salt & pepper, to taste

PROCEDURE

1. Combine the cooked turkey, carrots, celery, onions, potatoes, and dill in a large bowl—season with salt and pepper.

2. In a separate bowl, mix the turkey broth and heavy cream. Pour it over the turkey and vegetables, stirring thoroughly.

3. Fill clean jars with the filling, leaving a 1" headspace. Wipe jar rims clean with a damp cloth before placing lids on top and screwing on bands until finger tight.

4. Process jars in the pressure canner at 11 PSI for 90 minutes; adjust pressure for higher altitudes as needed.

5. After elapsed processing time, turn off the heat and let the canner cool and depressurize completely before removing the lid.

6. Carefully remove jars and let them cool on a wire rack for 12-24 hours. Check lids for proper seals before storing.

Maple-Glazed Turkey Tenderloins with Applesauce

PREPARATION TIME
25 Minutes

COOKING TIME
120 Minutes

JAR SIZE
Pint Sized

YELD
4 Jars

PRESSURE
11 PSI

INGREDIENTS

- 2 (about 1-pound each) turkey tenderloins
- 4 cups applesauce, preferably homemade
- 1/4 cup maple syrup
- 2 tbsp olive oil
- 1 tbsp apple cider vinegar
- 1 tsp ground cinnamon
- 1/2 tsp ground ginger
- 1/4 tsp ground cloves
- Salt & pepper, to taste

PROCEDURE

1. Pat the turkey tenderloins dry using paper towels, then season with salt and pepper.

2. Whisk maple syrup, olive oil, apple cider, cinnamon, ginger, and cloves in a small bowl.

3. Marinate the turkey tenderloins in the mixture within 15 minutes in the refrigerator.

4. Preheat your oven to 375°F. Line a baking sheet with foil.

5. Place the marinated turkey tenderloins on your baking sheet and bake within 30 minutes.

6. Baste with extra marinade every 10 minutes to keep them moist. Let it rest before slicing.

7. Warm the applesauce in your saucepan on low heat.

8. Fill clean jars with sliced maple-glazed turkey tenderloins and cover them with the applesauce, ensuring a headspace of ½".

9. Wipe the rims of the jars using a clean cloth, place lids plus rings on the jars, and tighten them finger-tight.

10. Process jars in the pressure canner at 11 PSI for 75 minutes; adjust pressure for higher altitudes as needed.

11. After elapsed processing time, turn off the heat, let the canner cool, and depressurize completely before removing the lid.

12. Carefully remove jars and let them cool on a wire rack for 12-24 hours. Check lids for proper seals before storing.

Lemon-Lime Turkey Breasts

PREPARATION TIME	COOKING TIME	JAR SIZE	YELD	PRESSURE
20 Min+Marinating time	75 Minutes	Pint Sized	6-8 Jars	11 PSI

INGREDIENTS

- 4 pounds boneless, skinless turkey breasts cut into 1-inch cubes
- 1/2 cup lemon juice
- 1/2 cup lime juice
- 1 tsp salt
- 1 tsp black pepper
- 2 tbsp olive oil
- 4 cloves garlic, minced

PROCEDURE

1. Combine lemon & lime juice, salt, pepper, olive oil, and garlic in a large bowl.

2. Add the turkey breasts, then mix well to ensure all pieces are coated. Cover the bowl using plastic wrap and refrigerate within 2 hours.

3. Once marinated, remove the turkey pieces and arrange them into clean, sterile jars.

4. Ladle the remaining marinade over each jar until they are covered with liquid, leaving a 1" headspace in each jar.

5. Wipe the rims of the jars using a clean cloth, place lids plus rings on the jars, and tighten them finger-tight.

6. Process jars in the pressure canner at 11 PSI for 75 minutes; adjust pressure for higher altitudes as needed.

7. After elapsed processing time, turn off the heat, let the canner cool, and depressurize completely before removing the lid.

8. Carefully remove jars and let them cool on a wire rack for 12-24 hours. Check lids for proper seals before storing.

Sun-Dried Tomato & Basil Turkey Meatballs

PREPARATION TIME

30 Minutes

COOKING TIME

95 Minutes

JAR SIZE

Pint Sized

YELD

4 Jars

PRESSURE

10 PSI

INGREDIENTS

- 2 pounds of ground turkey
- 1/2 cup sun-dried tomatoes, finely chopped
- 1/4 cup fresh basil, finely chopped
- 1/4 cup grated Parmesan cheese
- 2 cloves garlic, minced
- 1 large egg, beaten
- Salt & black pepper, to taste
- Olive oil, for sautéing

PROCEDURE

1. Combine the turkey, tomatoes, basil, Parmesan, garlic, egg, salt, and black pepper in your large bowl. Shape the mixture into golf ball-sized meatballs.

2. On medium heat in a pressure canning-compatible skillet with a little olive oil, sear the meatballs until they are browned on all sides.

3. Remove the meatballs and let them cool down.

4. Pack the cooled meatballs into clean and sterilized pint jars.

5. Wipe the rims of the jars using a clean cloth, place lids plus rings on the jars, and tighten them finger-tight.

6. Process jars in the pressure canner at 10 PSI for 75 minutes; adjust pressure for higher altitudes as needed.

7. After elapsed processing time, turn off the heat, let the canner cool, and depressurize completely before removing the lid.

8. Carefully remove jars and let them cool on a wire rack for 12-24 hours. Check lids for proper seals before storing.

Ranch-Style Turkey Chili

PREPARATION TIME

30 Minutes

COOKING TIME

85 Minutes

JAR SIZE

Pint Sized

YELD

6-8 Jars

PRESSURE

11 PSI

INGREDIENTS

- 2 pounds of ground turkey
- 2 tbsp olive oil
- 1 large onion, chopped
- 4 cloves garlic, minced
- 2 green bell peppers, chopped
- 2 red bell peppers, chopped
- 3 cups canned crushed tomatoes
- 1/4 cup chili powder
- 2 tbsp cumin
- 1 tbsp smoked paprika
- 1 tsp salt
- 1/2 tsp pepper
- 2 (15 oz) cans of black beans,
- 2 (15 oz) cans of pinto beans

PROCEDURE

1. In your large skillet, heat olive oil over medium heat. Add ground turkey and cook until browned. Transfer the turkey to your large bowl.

2. In the same skillet, sauté onions, garlic, and bell peppers until soft.

3. Add the vegetables to your turkey bowl. Stir in crushed tomatoes, chili powder, cumin, paprika, salt, and pepper.

4. Combine black beans(drained & rinsed) and pinto beans(drained & rinsed) in a separate bowl. Divide beans equally between clean and sterilized pint jars.

5. Fill each jar with chili mixture, leaving a 1" headspace. Remove air bubbles using a non-metallic spatula.

6. Wipe the rims of the jars using a clean cloth, place lids plus rings on the jars, and tighten them finger-tight.

7. Process jars in the pressure canner at 11 PSI for 75 minutes; adjust pressure for higher altitudes as needed.

8. After elapsed processing time, turn off the heat, let the canner cool, and depressurize completely before removing the lid.

9. Carefully remove jars and let them cool on a wire rack for 12-24 hours. Check lids for proper seals before storing.

Turkey Stroganoff

PREPARATION TIME
15 Minutes

COOKING TIME
95 Minutes

JAR SIZE
Pint Sized

YELD
4 Jars

PRESSURE
11 PSI

INGREDIENTS

- 2 pounds cooked, cubed turkey
- 1 medium onion, chopped
- 2 cloves garlic, minced
- 8 oz mushrooms, sliced
- 1 cup chicken broth
- 1 cup sour cream
- 1/4 cup all-purpose flour
- 2 tbsp vegetable oil
- Salt & pepper to taste

PROCEDURE

1. Heat the vegetable oil in your skillet over medium heat. Add the onions, garlic, and mushrooms. Cook within 5 minutes until softened.

2. Stir in the cooked turkey and cook within 5 minutes.

In your small bowl, whisk the flour and broth until smooth. Pour it into the skillet.

3. Let it boil, then adjust to low heat and simmer within 10 minutes or until the sauce has thickened.

4. Remove and let cool within a few minutes before stirring in sour cream.

5. Fill clean and sterilized jars with the Turkey Stroganoff mixture, leaving 1" headspace at the top of each jar.

6. Wipe the rims of the jars using a clean cloth, place lids plus rings on the jars, and tighten them finger-tight.

7. Process jars in the pressure canner at 11 PSI for 75 minutes; adjust pressure for higher altitudes as needed.

8. After elapsed processing time, turn off the heat, let the canner cool, and depressurize completely before removing the lid.

9. Carefully remove jars and let them cool on a wire rack for 12-24 hours. Check lids for proper seals before storing.

Turkey and Green Beans

PREPARATION TIME

30 Minutes

COOKING TIME

75 Minutes

JAR SIZE

Quart Sized

YELD

7-8 Jars

PRESSURE

11 PSI

INGREDIENTS

- 4 pounds of turkey meat, cut into 1-inch cubes
- 2 pounds fresh green beans, trimmed & sliced into 2-inch pieces
- 1 large onion, diced
- 4 cloves garlic, minced
- 2 cups chicken broth
- 1 tsp salt
- 1/2 tsp black pepper
- 1/2 tsp dried thyme

PROCEDURE

1. Mix the turkey meat, green beans, onion, and garlic in a large bowl.

2. Combine broth, salt, pepper, and thyme in a separate bowl.

3. Fill the sterilized jars with the turkey and green bean mixture, leaving a 1" headspace at the top of each jar.

4. Pour the seasoned broth over the mixture in each jar, maintaining a 1-inch headspace.

5. Wipe the rims of your jars with a clean cloth, place lids plus rings on the jars, and tighten them finger-tight.

6. Process jars in the pressure canner at 11 PSI for 75 minutes; adjust pressure for higher altitudes as needed.

7. After elapsed processing time, turn off the heat, let the canner cool, and depressurize completely before removing the lid.

8. Carefully remove jars and let them cool on a wire rack for 12-24 hours. Check lids for proper seals before storing.

PORK

Honey Mustard Pork Chops

PREPARATION TIME
15 Minutes

COOKING TIME
75 Minutes

JAR SIZE
Quart Sized

YELD
4 Jars

PRESSURE
11 PSI

INGREDIENTS

- 4 boneless pork chops, about 1" thick
- 1/4 cup honey
- 1/4 cup Dijon mustard
- 1/4 cup apple cider vinegar
- Salt & pepper, to taste
- 2 cloves of garlic, minced
- 1/2 tsp dried thyme

PROCEDURE

1. Combine the honey, Dijon, apple cider, garlic, and thyme in your small bowl. Set aside.

2. Flavor both sides of your pork chops using salt plus pepper.

3. Heat your large skillet over medium heat and sear the pork chops on each side within 2 minutes per side or until they turn golden brown.

4. Place the seared pork chops into your clean and sterilized jars, distributing them evenly.

5. Pour the honey mustard mixture over the pork chops, leaving a 1" headspace at the top.

6. Wipe the rims of your jars with a clean cloth, place lids plus rings on the jars, and tighten them finger-tight.

7. Process jars in the pressure canner at 11 PSI for 75 minutes; adjust pressure for higher altitudes as needed.

8. After elapsed processing time, turn off the heat, let the canner cool, and depressurize completely before removing the lid.

9. Carefully remove jars and let them cool on a wire rack for 12-24 hours. Check lids for proper seals before storing.

Stewed Pork with Potatoes

PREPARATION TIME
30 Minutes

COOKING TIME
115 Minutes

JAR SIZE
Quart Sized

YELD
4 Jars

PRESSURE
11 PSI

INGREDIENTS

- 2 pounds pork shoulder, sliced into 1" cubes
- 3 large potatoes, peeled and cubed
- 1 large onion, diced
- 2 cloves garlic, minced
- 1 cup carrots, chopped
- 1 cup green peas
- 1 cup tomato sauce
- 2 cups beef broth
- 1 tbsp olive oil
- Salt & pepper to taste

PROCEDURE

1. In your large pan, heat the olive oil over medium heat. Add the pork cubes, then cook until browned.

2. Add the onions and garlic, then cook within 5 minutes until the onions are translucent.

3. Add the potatoes, carrots, peas, tomato sauce, and broth—season with salt and pepper.

4. Let it boil, and adjust to a simmer within 30 minutes until the meat is tender.

5. Fill each clean and sterilized jar with the stewed pork mixture leaving a 1" headspace at the top of each jar.

6. Wipe the rims of your jars with a clean cloth, place lids plus rings on the jars, and tighten them finger-tight.

7. Process jars in the pressure canner at 11 PSI for 75 minutes; adjust pressure for higher altitudes as needed.

8. After elapsed processing time, turn off the heat, let the canner cool, and depressurize completely before removing the lid.

9. Carefully remove jars and let them cool on a wire rack for 12-24 hours. Check lids for proper seals before storing.

Spiced Apple Pork

PREPARATION TIME	COOKING TIME	JAR SIZE	YELD	PRESSURE
30 Minutes	75 Minutes	Pint Sized	6-8 Jars	11 PSI

INGREDIENTS

- 4 pounds of pork shoulder, cubed
- 4 cups apples, peeled and chopped
- 1 cup onion, diced
- 1/2 cup brown sugar
- 1/4 cup apple cider vinegar

- 1 tbsp cinnamon
- 1 tsp nutmeg
- Salt & pepper to taste
- Boiling water for canning

PROCEDURE

1. Combine the pork, apples, onions, brown sugar, apple cider, cinnamon, nutmeg, salt, and pepper in a large bowl.

2. Fill each clean and sterilized jar with the pork mixture, leaving a 1" headspace at the top of each jar.

3. Pour boiling water over the pork mixture until it covers the meat, maintaining a 1" headspace.

4. Wipe the rims of the jars using a clean cloth, place lids plus rings on the jars, and tighten them finger-tight.

5. Process jars in the pressure canner at 11 PSI for 75 minutes; adjust pressure for higher altitudes as needed.

6. After elapsed processing time, turn off the heat, let the canner cool, and depressurize completely before removing the lid.

7. Carefully remove jars and let them cool on a wire rack for 12-24 hours. Check lids for proper seals before storing.

Apricot Glazed Pork Tenderloin

PREPARATION TIME

15 Min+Marinating time

COOKING TIME

75 Minutes

JAR SIZE

Half Pint Sized

YELD

6 Jars

PRESSURE

10 PSI

INGREDIENTS

- 2 pounds pork tenderloin, trimmed any silver skin & cut into small cubes
- 1 cup apricot preserves
- 2 tbsp soy sauce
- 2 tbsp minced garlic
- 1/4 cup balsamic vinegar
- Salt & pepper, to taste

PROCEDURE

1. Season the pork tenderloin with salt plus pepper.

2. Mix the apricot preserves, soy sauce, garlic, and balsamic vinegar in your small bowl.

3. Place the pork tenderloin in your large bowl and pour the glaze over it, stirring to distribute the glaze evenly.

4. Allow the pork tenderloin cubes to marinate in the refrigerator within 30 minutes.

5. Evenly pack the marinated pork tenderloin cubes into clean and sterilized half-pint mason jars, leaving 1" of headspace.

6. Wipe the rims of the jars using a clean cloth, place lids plus rings on the jars, and tighten them finger-tight.

7. Process jars in the pressure canner at 10 PSI for 75 minutes; adjust pressure for higher altitudes as needed.

8. After elapsed processing time, turn off the heat, let the canner cool, and depressurize completely before removing the lid.

9. Carefully remove jars and let them cool on a wire rack for 12-24 hours. Check lids for proper seals before storing.

BBQ Pulled Pork

PREPARATION TIME

30 Minutes

COOKING TIME

90 Minutes

JAR SIZE

Quart Sized

YELD

2-3 Jars

PRESSURE

10 PSI

INGREDIENTS

- 4 pounds of pork shoulder, cut into chunks
- 2 cups BBQ sauce
- 1 cup apple cider vinegar
- 1/2 cup brown sugar
- 1 tbsp Worcestershire sauce
- 1 tsp paprika
- 1 tsp garlic powder
- Salt & pepper, to taste

PROCEDURE

1. Mix the BBQ sauce, apple cider vinegar, brown sugar, Worcestershire sauce, paprika, garlic powder, salt, and pepper in your large bowl.

2. Add the pork chunks, ensuring that each piece is well coated. Marinate in your refrigerator within 2 hours or overnight for better flavor infusion.

3. Remove the marinated pork from your refrigerator and pack it tightly into the sterilized quart jars with some sauce, leaving 1" of headspace.

4. Wipe the rims of the jars using a clean cloth, place lids plus rings on the jars, and tighten them finger-tight. Process jars in the pressure canner at 10 PSI for 90 minutes; adjust pressure for higher altitudes as needed.

5. After elapsed processing time, turn off the heat, let the canner cool, and depressurize completely before removing the lid.

6. Carefully remove jars and let them cool on a wire rack for 12-24 hours. Check lids for proper seals before storing.

Spanish Garlic and Paprika Pork Stew

PREPARATION TIME
30 Minutes

COOKING TIME
2 Hours 30 Minutes

JAR SIZE
Pint Sized

YELD
4 Jars

PRESSURE
10 PSI

INGREDIENTS

- 2 pounds pork shoulder, sliced into 1" cubes
- 4 cloves garlic, minced
- 1 large onion, chopped
- 1 red bell pepper, chopped
- 1 green bell pepper, chopped
- 1/4 cup olive oil
- 1/4 cup sweet paprika
- 2 tsp smoked paprika
- 2 tsp salt
- 1 tsp black pepper
- 1/2 tsp thyme leaves
- 1 bay leaf
- 14 oz canned diced tomatoes
- 3 cups beef broth

PROCEDURE

1. Toss the cubed pork, garlic, sweet & smoked paprika, salt, and black pepper in your large bowl. Set aside within 20 minutes.

2. Heat the olive oil in your large heavy-bottomed pot over medium heat. Add the pork cubes, then cook until browned on all sides. Remove and set aside.

3. In your same pot, add the onions and peppers. Cook within 5 minutes until softened.

4. Return the browned pork to your pot with drained tomatoes, broth, thyme, and bay leaf.

5. Let it boil, and adjust to a simmer within 60 minutes to allow flavors to meld. Remove and discard the bay leaf.

6. Fill hot sterilized jars with stew, leaving about a 1" headspace.

7. Wipe the rims of the jars using a clean cloth, place lids plus rings on the jars, and tighten them finger-tight.

8. Process jars in the pressure canner at 10 PSI for 75 minutes; adjust pressure for higher altitudes as needed.

9. After elapsed processing time, turn off the heat, let the canner cool, and depressurize completely before removing the lid.

10. Carefully remove jars and let them cool on a wire rack for 12-24 hours. Check lids for proper seals before storing.

Spanish Garlic and Paprika Pork Stew

 PREPARATION TIME

 **COOKING TIME**

 JAR SIZE

 YELD

 PRESSURE

30 Minutes   100 Minutes   Quart Sized   4 Jars   10 PSI

INGREDIENTS

- 4 pounds pork roast, trimmed any excess fat
- 1/2 cup olive oil
- 6 cloves garlic, minced
- 1/4 cup fresh sage leaves, chopped
- 2 tsp coarse salt
- 1 tsp ground black pepper
- 1 cup chicken or vegetable broth

PROCEDURE

1. Combine the garlic, sage, salt, and black pepper in your small bowl.

2. Rub the pork roast with garlic-sage mixture all over its surface.

3. In your large skillet, heat the olive oil over medium-high heat. Brown the pork roast on all sides within 4-5 minutes each side until it has a nice crust.

4. Remove the pork and let it rest for 10 minutes before slicing it into 1-inch-thick pieces.

5. Pour the broth into the now-empty skillet, scraping up any browned bits.

6. Pack the sliced pork roast into sterilized jars, leaving 1" of headspace at the top of each jar.

7. Pour warmed broth over the pork in each jar until it reaches about an inch from the top, ensuring all pork is covered.

8. Wipe the rims of your jars with a clean cloth, place lids plus rings on the jars, and tighten them finger-tight.

9. Process jars in the pressure canner at 10 PSI for 90 minutes; adjust pressure for higher altitudes as needed.

10. After elapsed processing time, turn off the heat, let the canner cool, and depressurize completely before removing the lid.

11. Carefully remove jars and let them cool on a wire rack for 12-24 hours. Check lids for proper seals before storing.

Sticky Asian-Style Pork Ribs

PREPARATION TIME
30 Min+Marinating time

COOKING TIME
60 Minutes

JAR SIZE
Pint Sized

YELD
4 Jars

PRESSURE
11 PSI

INGREDIENTS

- 2 pounds of pork ribs
- 1/2 cup soy sauce
- 1/2 cup hoisin sauce
- 1/4 cup honey
- 3 tbsp rice vinegar
- 3 cloves garlic, minced
- 1 tbsp fresh ginger, grated
- 2 tsp sesame oil
- 1 tsp Chinese five-spice powder

PROCEDURE

1. Mix the soy sauce, hoisin, honey, rice vinegar, garlic, ginger, sesame oil, and Chinese five-spice powder in a bowl.

2. Place the pork ribs in your gallon-sized resealable plastic bag. Pour the marinade over your ribs and massage it into the ribs, ensuring they're fully coated.

3. Refrigerate and allow the ribs to marinate within 2 hours.

4. Pack the marinated pork ribs tightly into each sterilized pint jar. Pour any remaining marinade into each jar.

5. Wipe the rims of your jars using a clean cloth, place lids plus rings on them, and tighten them finger-tight.

6. Process jars in the pressure canner at 11 PSI for 60 minutes; adjust pressure for higher altitudes as needed.

7. After elapsed processing time, turn off the heat, let the canner cool, and depressurize completely before removing the lid.

8. Carefully remove jars and let them cool on a wire rack for 12-24 hours. Check lids for proper seals before storing.

Caribbean Coconut Curry Pork

PREPARATION TIME

30 Minutes

COOKING TIME

120 Minutes

JAR SIZE

Pint Sized

YELD

4 Jars

PRESSURE

11 PSI

INGREDIENTS

- 2 pounds pork shoulder, cubed
- 1 (14 oz) can coconut milk
- 1 large onion, chopped
- 2 small carrots, chopped
- 1 red bell pepper, chopped
- 1 green bell pepper, chopped
- 3 cloves garlic, minced
- 2 tbsp curry powder
- 1 tbsp vegetable oil
- Salt & pepper to taste

PROCEDURE

1. Heat the vegetable oil in your large skillet over medium heat. Add the onions, garlic, and carrots. Cook until the onions are translucent.

2. Add the cubed pork, then cook until browned on all sides. Stir in curry powder and cook for a couple of minutes.

3. Stir in coconut milk, salt, and pepper. Let it boil and simmer within 1 hour or until the pork is tender. Add the bell peppers during the last 20 minutes of cooking.

4. Spoon the prepared Coconut Curry Pork mixture into your clean and sterilized jars, leaving 1" headspace at the top of each jar.

5. Wipe the rims of the jars using a clean cloth, place lids plus rings on the jars, and tighten them finger-tight. Process jars in the pressure canner at 11 PSI for 75 minutes; adjust pressure for higher altitudes as needed.

6. After elapsed processing time, turn off the heat, let the canner cool, and depressurize completely before removing the lid.

7. Carefully remove jars and let them cool on a wire rack for 12-24 hours. Check lids for proper seals before storing.

Kalua Pork

PREPARATION TIME

30 Minutes

COOKING TIME

90 Minutes

JAR SIZE

Pint Sized

YELD

6-8 Jars

PRESSURE

10 PSI

INGREDIENTS

- 4 pounds of pork shoulder or butt, trimmed any excess fat & cut into 2" cubes
- 2 tbsp liquid smoke
- 1 tbsp Hawaiian sea salt
- 1 cup water

PROCEDURE

1. Place the cubed pork in your large bowl. Add liquid smoke and sea salt. Toss until the pork is evenly coated.

2. Pack the seasoned pork tightly into clean and sterilized pint-sized jars, leaving a 1" headspace at the top.

3. Wipe the rims of your jars with a clean cloth, place lids plus rings on the jars, and tighten them finger-tight.

4. Process jars in the pressure canner at 11 PSI for 90 minutes; adjust pressure for higher altitudes as needed.

5. After elapsed processing time, turn off the heat, let the canner cool, and depressurize completely before removing the lid.

6. Carefully remove jars and let them cool on a wire rack for 12-24 hours. Check lids for proper seals before storing.

Lemon Herb Pork Chops

PREPARATION TIME	COOKING TIME	JAR SIZE	YELD	PRESSURE
30 Minutes	81 Minutes	Pint Sized	4 Jars	11 PSI

INGREDIENTS

- 4 bone-in pork chops (about 1-inch thick)
- 1 tbsp olive oil
- Salt & pepper, to taste
- 1/2 cup fresh lemon juice
- Zest of one lemon
- 2 cloves garlic, minced
- 1 tsp dried basil
- 1 tsp dried oregano
- 1 tsp dried thyme
- 1 cup chicken broth

PROCEDURE

1. Flavor pork chops on both sides with salt and pepper.

2. Heat olive oil in your large skillet over medium-high heat. Brown the pork chops on both sides within 2-3 minutes per side. Remove and set aside.

3. Whisk lemon juice, zest, garlic, basil, oregano, thyme, and broth in a small bowl.

4. Place the pork chops in your clean and sterilized pint-sized jars, fitting one chop per jar.

5. Pour the lemon herb mixture over pork chops, leaving a 1" headspace in each jar.

6. Wipe the rims of the jars using a clean cloth, place lids plus rings on the jars, and tighten them finger-tight.

7. Process jars in the pressure canner at 11 PSI for 75 minutes; adjust pressure for higher altitudes as needed.

8. After elapsed processing time, turn off the heat, let the canner cool, and depressurize completely before removing the lid.

9. Carefully remove jars and let them cool on a wire rack for 12-24 hours. Check lids for proper seals before storing.

Pineapple Teriyaki Pork Loin

PREPARATION TIME
20 Min+Marinating time

COOKING TIME
75 Minutes

JAR SIZE
Pint Sized

YELD
3-4 Jars

PRESSURE
10 PSI

INGREDIENTS

- 2 pounds pork loin, cubed
- 1/2 cup teriyaki sauce
- 1/4 cup soy sauce
- 1/4 cup brown sugar
- 1 small (8 ounce) can of crushed pineapple, undrained
- 1 medium onion, diced
- 2 cloves garlic, minced

PROCEDURE

1. Combine teriyaki sauce, soy sauce, brown sugar, pineapple (with juice), onion, and garlic in a large bowl.

2. Add the cubed pork loin, and mix well to ensure all pieces are coated. Allow the pork to marinate in your refrigerator within 1 hour.

3. Pack the marinated pork cubes and remaining marinade into clean and sterilized pint-sized jars, leaving 1" headspace.

4. Wipe the rims of the jars using a clean cloth, place lids plus rings on the jars, and tighten them finger-tight.

5. Process jars in the pressure canner at 10 PSI for 75 minutes; adjust pressure for higher altitudes as needed.

6. After elapsed processing time, turn off the heat, let the canner cool, and depressurize completely before removing the lid.

7. Carefully remove jars and let them cool on a wire rack for 12-24 hours. Check lids for proper seals before storing.

Pork Vegetable Casserole

PREPARATION TIME
30 Minutes

COOKING TIME
150 Minutes

JAR SIZE
Quart Sized

YELD
4 Jars

PRESSURE
10 PSI

INGREDIENTS

- 2 pounds pork shoulder, cubed
- 4 medium carrots, sliced
- 2 large potatoes, cubed
- 1 large onion, chopped
- 4 cloves garlic, minced
- 1/4 cup vegetable oil
- 2 cups chicken broth
- 1 (14.5 oz) can of diced tomatoes
- 1 tsp salt
- 1/2 tsp black pepper
- 1 tsp dried thyme
- 1 tsp dried rosemary

PROCEDURE

1. In your large skillet, heat the oil over medium-high heat. Brown the pork cubes on all sides and set aside.

2. Add onions and garlic to your skillet and cook until softened.

3. Combine the pork, onions, garlic, carrots, potatoes, broth, tomatoes, salt, pepper, thyme, and rosemary in your pressure canner.

4. Place the lid and lock it in place. Set at 10 PSI, adjust heat as needed to maintain a steady pressure, and cook for 75 minutes.

5. Turn off the heat, then let the pressure canner depressurize completely before removing the lid.

6. Carefully transfer the hot pork casserole mixture into clean and sterilized quart jars, leaving 1" of headspace at the top.

7. Wipe the rims of your jars with a clean cloth, place lids plus rings on the jars, and tighten them finger-tight.

8. Process jars in the pressure canner at 10 PSI for 75 minutes; adjust pressure for higher altitudes as needed.

9. After elapsed processing time, turn off the heat, let the canner cool, and depressurize completely before removing the lid.

10. Carefully remove jars and let them cool on a wire rack for 12-24 hours. Check lids for proper seals before storing.

Maple Bourbon Pork Ribs

PREPARATION TIME

30 Min+Marinating Time

COOKING TIME

100 Minutes

JAR SIZE

Quart Sized

YELD

3-4 Jars

PRESSURE

10 PSI

INGREDIENTS

- 4 pounds of pork ribs, cut into 3-inch strips
- 1 cup maple syrup
- 1 cup bourbon
- 1/2 cup apple cider vinegar
- 1/4 cup grainy mustard
- 1/4 cup Worcestershire sauce
- 2 tbsp soy sauce
- 3 cloves garlic, minced
- Salt & pepper to taste

PROCEDURE

1. Begin by seasoning the pork ribs with salt and pepper.

2. Mix maple syrup, bourbon, apple cider, mustard, Worcestershire, soy sauce, and garlic in your large bowl.

3. Add the seasoned ribs to the marinade and refrigerate within 2 hours, turning them often to ensure they're well-coated.

4. Remove the ribs from the marinade and set aside. Pour the marinade into your saucepan and simmer over medium heat. Cook within 10 minutes until it thickens slightly.

5. Start packing marinated pork ribs firmly into the clean and sterilized jars, leaving about an inch of headspace on top.

6. Pour the thickened marinade over the ribs in each jar until they are covered with a 1/2" of liquid left on top as headspace.

7. Wipe the rims of your jars with a clean cloth, place lids plus rings on the jars, and tighten them finger-tight.

8. Process jars in the pressure canner at 10 PSI for 90 minutes; adjust pressure for higher altitudes as needed.

9. After elapsed processing time, turn off the heat, let the canner cool, and depressurize completely before removing the lid.

10. Carefully remove jars and let them cool on a wire rack for 12-24 hours. Check lids for proper seals before storing.

Chipotle Pork and Pepper Stew

PREPARATION TIME
30 Minutes

COOKING TIME
150 Minutes

JAR SIZE
Pint Sized

YELD
6-8 Jars

PRESSURE
11 PSI

INGREDIENTS

- 2 pounds pork shoulder, sliced into 1" cubes
- 1 large onion, chopped
- 3 garlic cloves, minced
- 2 tbsp olive oil
- 1 tbsp chipotle powder or smoked paprika
- 2 tsp ground cumin
- 1 tsp salt
- 1/2 tsp black pepper
- 2 cups diced tomatoes
- 3 medium red, green, & yellow bell peppers, seeded and chopped
- 1 cup corn kernels
- 4 cups low-sodium chicken broth

PROCEDURE

1. In your large skillet, heat the olive oil over medium-high heat. Add the onion, garlic, and pork cubes. Cook until the pork is browned and the onions are softened.

2. Add the chipotle powder, cumin, salt, and black pepper. Stir well.

3. Add the tomatoes, bell peppers, corn, and broth. Let it boil.

4. Adjust to medium-low heat and simmer within 1 hour until the pork is cooked through.

5. Ladle the hot stew into clean and sterilized pint jars, leaving 1" headspace.

6. Wipe the rims of the jars using a clean cloth, place lids plus rings on the jars, and tighten them finger-tight.

7. Process jars in the pressure canner at 11 PSI for 75 minutes; adjust pressure for higher altitudes as needed.

8. After elapsed processing time, turn off the heat, let the canner cool, and depressurize completely before removing the lid.

9. Carefully remove jars and let them cool on a wire rack for 12-24 hours. Check lids for proper seals before storing.

Traditional Pork and Beans

 PREPARATION TIME

30 Min+Soaking Time

 COOKING TIME

115 Minutes

 JAR SIZE

Pint Sized

YELD

6 Jars

 PRESSURE

10 PSI

INGREDIENTS

- 1-pound dry navy beans, soaked in water overnight, drained & rinsed
- ½-pound salt pork or bacon diced
- 4 cups water
- 1/4 cup molasses

- 1/4 cup ketchup
- 2 tbsp brown sugar
- 2 tsp dry mustard
- 1 tsp salt

PROCEDURE

1. Cover the beans with enough water in your large saucepan and let it boil. Cook within 30 minutes, then drain.

2. In your separate pot, add the bacon and cook until browned.

3. Combine beans, pork, water, molasses, ketchup, brown sugar, mustard, and salt in your large saucepan.

4. Heat the bean mixture to boiling within 5 minutes.

5. Ladle hot beans and sauce into your sterilized jars, leaving a 1" headspace.

6. Wipe the rims of the jars using a clean cloth, place lids plus rings on the jars, and tighten them finger-tight.

7. Process jars In the pressure canner at 10 PSI for 75 minutes; adjust pressure for higher altitudes as needed.

8. After elapsed processing time, turn off the heat, let the canner cool, and depressurize completely before removing the lid.

9. Carefully remove jars and let them cool on a wire rack for 12-24 hours. Check lids for proper seals before storing.

Green Chile & Lime Carnitas

PREPARATION TIME	COOKING TIME	JAR SIZE	YELD	PRESSURE
20 Minutes	135 Minutes	Pint Sized	6 Jars	10 PSI

INGREDIENTS

- 3 pounds pork shoulder, cut into 2-inch cubes
- 1 tbsp olive oil
- 1 large onion, chopped
- 3 cloves garlic, minced
- 1 tsp ground cumin
- 1 tsp dried oregano
- 2 cups green chile sauce
- 2 limes, juiced
- Salt & pepper, to taste

PROCEDURE

1. Set your pressure cooker to the sauté setting and add the olive oil.

2. Season the pork cubes with salt, pepper, cumin, and oregano.

3. Add the pork to your pressure cooker and brown on all sides. Remove and set aside.

4. Add the onions to your pot and cook within 5 minutes until softened. Add the garlic and cook within 1 minute.

5. Return the browned pork to your pot with 1/2 green chile sauce and lime juice.

6. Attach the lid to the pressure cooker and set it to high pressure for 45 minutes.

7. Once done cooking, release pressure naturally within 15 minutes before manually releasing any remaining pressure.

8. Transfer cooked pork pieces into sterilized jars evenly.

9. Stir the remaining green chile sauce into the cooking liquid left in your pressure cooker, then let it simmer for 5 minutes or until slightly thickened.

10. Pour green chile sauce mixture over pork in each jar, leaving a ½" headspace.

11. Wipe the rims of yur jars using a clean cloth, place lids plus rings on the jars, and tighten them finger-tight.

12. Process jars in the pressure canner at 11 PSI for 75 minutes; adjust pressure for higher altitudes as needed.

13. After elapsed processing time, turn off the heat, let the canner cool, and depressurize completely before removing the lid.

14. Carefully remove jars and let them cool on a wire rack for 12-24 hours. Check lids for proper seals before storing.

Pork Chops in White Wine Sauce

PREPARATION TIME

20 Minutes

COOKING TIME

100 Minutes

JAR SIZE

Quart Sized

YELD

4 Jars

PRESSURE

10 PSI

INGREDIENTS

- 6 pork chops, boneless, about 1-inch thick
- Salt & pepper, to taste
- 2 tbsp olive oil
- 1 medium onion, chopped
- 3 cloves garlic, minced
- 1 cup white wine
- 1 cup chicken broth
- 2 tbsp Dijon mustard
- 2 tbsp fresh parsley, chopped
- 1 tsp dried thyme

PROCEDURE

1. Flavor both sides of the pork chops using salt plus pepper.

2. Preheat your pressure cooker over medium heat.

3. Add olive oil to your pressure cooker, then add the pork chops, then sear on both sides until golden brown. Remove and set aside.

4. Add the onion and garlic to your pressure cooker and cook within 3 minutes until softened.

5. Pour the white wine and deglaze to loosen any browned bits. Simmer within 1 minute. Stir in broth, Dijon mustard, parsley, plus thyme.

6. Return the seared pork chops to your pressure cooker and submerge them in the sauce.

7. Lock your pressure cooker and bring it to high pressure.

8. Cook at high pressure within 25 minutes before quick-releasing the pressure.

9. Carefully ladle the hot mixture equally into sterilized quart-sized jars, leaving 1" of headspace.

10. Wipe the rims of the jars using a clean cloth, place lids plus rings on the jars, and tighten them finger-tight.

11. Process jars in the pressure canner at 11 PSI for 75 minutes; adjust pressure for higher altitudes as needed.

12. After elapsed processing time, turn off the heat, let the canner cool, and depressurize completely before removing the lid.

13. Carefully remove jars and let them cool on a wire rack for 12-24 hours. Check lids for proper seals before storing.

WILD GAME

Teriyaki Glazed Quail

PREPARATION TIME

30 Minutes

COOKING TIME

60 Minutes

JAR SIZE

Quart Sized

YELD

6 Jars

PRESSURE

11 PSI

INGREDIENTS

- 12 whole quails, cleaned
- 1 cup teriyaki sauce
- 3 tbsp honey
- 2 tbsp sesame oil
- 1 tbsp minced garlic
- 1 tbsp minced ginger
- 1/4 cup chopped green onions
- Salt & pepper to taste

PROCEDURE

1. Pat the quails dry and set aside.

2. Mix teriyaki sauce, honey, sesame oil, garlic, ginger, and green onions in a small bowl.

3. Season each quail with salt and pepper. Pour the teriyaki glaze mixture over the quails, ensuring they are evenly coated.

4. Marinate the quails in the refrigerator within 1 hour. Preheat your pressure canner to medium heat.

5. Place the marinated quails in quart-sized sterilized jars, leaving 1" of headspace at the top.

6. Pour any remaining marinade over the quails in the jars.

7. Wipe the rims of your jars with a clean cloth, place lids plus rings on the jars, and tighten them finger-tight.

8. Process jars in the pressure canner at 11 PSI for 60 minutes; adjust pressure for higher altitudes as needed.

9. After elapsed processing time, turn off the heat, let the canner cool, and depressurize completely before removing the lid.

10. Carefully remove jars and let them cool on a wire rack for 12-24 hours. Check lids for proper seals before storing.

Thai Red Curry Duck

PREPARATION TIME
30 Minutes

COOKING TIME
60 Minutes

JAR SIZE
Pint Sized

YELD
6 Jars

PRESSURE
11 PSI

INGREDIENTS

- 2 pounds duck, cut into small pieces
- 3 cups coconut milk
- 1/2 cup Thai red curry paste
- 2 cups water
- 2 tbsp fish sauce
- 2 tbsp sugar
- 1/2 cup bamboo shoots, sliced
- 1/2 cup cherry tomatoes, halved
- 1/4 cup fresh Thai basil leaves
- Salt to taste

PROCEDURE

1. Heat your large pot over medium heat and add the coconut milk. Stir in the Thai red curry paste until well combined.

2. Add the duck pieces and cook within 5 minutes, stirring often until the duck is evenly coated with the curry paste.

3. Pour in the water, fish sauce, and sugar. Let it boil, then adjust to low heat.

4. Cover and simmer within 45 minutes or until the duck is tender.

5. Stir in the bamboo shoots and cherry tomatoes, then cook within 5 minutes. Remove and add salt if needed. Stir in basil leaves.

6. Ladle the Thai Red Curry Duck mixture into clean and sanitized jars, leaving about ½" headspace.

7. Wipe the rims of your jars with a clean cloth, place lids plus rings on the jars, and tighten them finger-tight.

8. Process jars in the pressure canner at 11 PSI for 60 minutes; adjust pressure for higher altitudes as needed.

9. After elapsed processing time, turn off the heat, let the canner cool, and depressurize completely before removing the lid.

10. Carefully remove jars and let them cool on a wire rack for 12-24 hours. Check lids for proper seals before storing.

Dove Hunter

PREPARATION TIME

30 Minutes

COOKING TIME

160 Minutes

JAR SIZE

Pint Sized

YELD

6 Jars

PRESSURE

11 PSI

INGREDIENTS

- 4 pounds dove breasts, bone-in and skinless
- Salt & pepper to taste
- 2 tbsp olive oil
- 1 cup onion, finely chopped
- 1 cup celery, finely chopped
- 1 cup carrots, finely chopped
- 3 cloves garlic, minced
- 1 cup mushroom, sliced
- 1 tsp basil
- 2 (28 oz each) cans of crushed tomatoes
- 1 tsp oregano
- 1/2 tsp thyme

PROCEDURE

1. Season the dove breast with salt plus pepper. Brown them in olive oil over medium heat in your pressure cooker. Remove and keep them aside.

2. Add onions, celery, carrots, garlic, and mushrooms in the same pressure cooker. Cook vegetables until they turn soft.

3. Add crushed tomatoes and stir well. Add oregano, basil, and thyme to the mixture.

4. Place the cooked dove breasts in your pressure cooker with the tomato mixture.

5. Close the pressure cooker properly and cook for 60 minutes at a PRESSURE of 11 PSI.

6. Once cooking is done, carefully open the pressure cooker according to its instructions.

7. Fill sterilized quart jars with the dove cacciatore mixture leaving a ½" headspace.

8. Wipe the rims of your jars with a clean cloth, place lids plus rings on the jars, and tighten them finger-tight.

9. Process jars in the pressure canner at 11 PSI for 90 minutes; adjust pressure for higher altitudes as needed.

10. After elapsed processing time, turn off the heat, let the canner cool, and depressurize completely before removing the lid.

11. Carefully remove jars and let them cool on a wire rack for 12-24 hours. Check lids for proper seals before storing.

Wild Duck Curry

PREPARATION TIME	COOKING TIME	JAR SIZE	YELD	PRESSURE
30 Minutes	80 Minutes	Pint Sized	6 Jars	11 PSI

INGREDIENTS

- 2 wild ducks, cleaned and cut into pieces
- 2 tbsp vegetable oil
- 1 large onion, chopped
- 3 cloves garlic, minced
- 1 tbsp ginger, minced
- 2 tbsp curry powder
- 1 tsp turmeric powder
- 1 tsp cumin powder
- 1/2 tsp chili powder (optional)
- 2 cups coconut milk
- 2 cups water
- 3 tbsp lime juice
- Salt to taste

PROCEDURE

1. In your pressure cooker, heat the vegetable oil on medium heat. Sauté the onions, garlic, and ginger until soft and fragrant.

2. Add the duck pieces and brown them on all sides.

3. Stir in the curry powder, turmeric powder, cumin powder, chili powder (if using), and salt until the duck pieces are evenly coated.

4. Pour the coconut milk, water, and lime juice. Mix well. Lock the pressure cooker lid and cook on high pressure for 1 hour.

5. After one hour, release the pressure from the cooker according to the manufacturer's instructions. Carefully remove the lid and ensure the duck is tender and fully cooked.

6. Ladle the hot curry into your sterilized jars, leaving a ½" headspace.

7. Wipe the rims of your jars with a clean cloth, place lids plus rings on the jars, and tighten them finger-tight.

8. Process jars in the pressure canner at 11 PSI for 75 minutes; adjust pressure for higher altitudes as needed.

9. After elapsed processing time, turn off the heat, let the canner cool, and depressurize completely before removing the lid.

10. Carefully remove jars and let them cool on a wire rack for 12-24 hours. Check lids for proper seals before storing.

Duck Stew with Mushrooms and Vegetables

 PREPARATION TIME

30 Minutes

 COOKING TIME

175 Minutes

 JAR SIZE

Pint Sized

 YELD

6 Jars

PRESSURE

11 PSI

INGREDIENTS

- 2 pounds duck, cut into small pieces
- 1-pound fresh mushrooms, sliced
- 2 carrots, chopped
- 2 stalks of celery, chopped
- 1 large onion, chopped
- 3 cloves garlic, minced
- 4 cups vegetable broth
- 2 cups red wine
- 2 tbsp tomato paste
- 1 bay leaf
- Salt and pepper to taste

PROCEDURE

1. In your large skillet over medium heat, brown the duck pieces on all sides. Once browned, transfer them to a pressure canning pot.

2. In the same skillet, sauté the mushrooms until they start to brown.

3. Add the sautéed mushrooms, carrots, celery, onion, and garlic to your pressure canning pot with the duck.

4. Stir in the broth, red wine, tomato paste, and bay leaf—season with salt and pepper.

5. Place the lid on your pressure canner and lock it in place. Let it boil over medium-high heat.

6. Cook at 11PSI for 1 hour and 30 minutes. Carefully release the pressure using the manufacturer's instructions before opening the lid.

7. Ladle the hot stew into sterilized jars, leaving a ½" headspace at the top.

8. Wipe the rims of your jars with a clean cloth, place lids plus rings on the jars, and tighten them finger-tight.

9. Process jars in the pressure canner at 11 PSI for 75 minutes; adjust pressure for higher altitudes as needed.

10. After elapsed processing time, turn off the heat, let the canner cool, and depressurize completely before removing the lid.

11. Carefully remove jars and let them cool on a wire rack for 12-24 hours. Check lids for proper seals before storing.

Orange-Honey Duck Confit

PREPARATION TIME	COOKING TIME	JAR SIZE	YELD	PRESSURE
30 Min+Marinating Time	60 Minutes	Half Pint Sized	6 Jars	11 PSI

INGREDIENTS

- 4 duck legs
- 2 cups duck fat, melted
- 1/2 cup honey
- Zest of 2 oranges
- 2 tbsp fresh orange juice
- 1/2 cup kosher salt
- 2 tsp black peppercorns, crushed
- 4 fresh thyme sprigs
- 4 garlic cloves, crushed

PROCEDURE

1. Combine the duck legs, salt, peppercorns, thyme, and garlic in a large bowl. Mix well and refrigerate within 12 hours.

2. Preheat your pressure canner to medium heat.

3. Rinse the excess salt mixture from the duck legs and dry them with paper towels.

4. Heat your large skillet over medium heat and gently sear the duck legs on all sides until golden. Remove.

5. Combine the dissolved duck fat, honey, zest, and orange juice in another bowl.

6. Place the seared duck legs in your sterilized half-pint jars, leaving about 1" headspace in each jar.

7. Pour the orange-honey mixture over each duck leg until completely submerged in liquid.

8. Wipe the rims of your jars with a clean cloth, place lids plus rings on the jars, and tighten them finger-tight.

9. Process jars in the pressure canner at 11 PSI for 60 minutes; adjust pressure for higher altitudes as needed.

10. After elapsed processing time, turn off the heat, let the canner cool, and depressurize completely before removing the lid.

11. Carefully remove jars and let them cool on a wire rack for 12-24 hours. Check lids for proper seals before storing.

Duck Gumbo

PREPARATION TIME

30 Minutes

COOKING TIME

85 Minutes

JAR SIZE

Pint Sized

YELD

6 Jars

PRESSURE

11 PSI

INGREDIENTS

- 2 pounds of duck meat, cubed
- 1/4 cup vegetable oil
- 1/4 cup all-purpose flour
- 1 large onion, chopped
- 1 green bell pepper, chopped
- 2 celery stalks, chopped
- 4 cloves garlic, minced
- 6 cups chicken stock
- 1-pound sliced okra
- 1 tbsp Creole seasoning
- 2 tsp thyme leaves
- Salt & pepper to taste

PROCEDURE

1. In your large pot over medium heat, combine the oil and flour. Cook within 5 minutes, stirring to form a roux.

2. Add the onion, bell pepper, celery, and garlic. Cook within 5 minutes until the vegetables begin to soften. Stir in the duck meat, then cook until browned.

3. Add the chicken stock and okra. Let it boil, adjust to low heat, and simmer within 30 minutes. Stir in Creole seasoning, thyme, salt, and pepper.

4. Ladle hot gumbo into pint jars, leaving a 1" headspace in each jar.

5. Wipe the rims of your jars with a clean cloth, place lids plus rings on the jars, and tighten them finger-tight.

6. Process jars in the pressure canner at 11 PSI for 45 minutes; adjust pressure for higher altitudes as needed.

7. After elapsed processing time, turn off the heat, let the canner cool, and depressurize completely before removing the lid.

8. Carefully remove jars and let them cool on a wire rack for 12-24 hours. Check lids for proper seals before storing.

Hen with Orange-Pomegranate Preserves

PREPARATION TIME

30 Minutes

COOKING TIME

150 Minutes

JAR SIZE

Pint Sized

YELD

6 Jars

PRESSURE

11 PSI

INGREDIENTS

- 3 Cornish hens, halved and de-boned
- 1 tsp ground cumin
- 1 tsp ground coriander
- 1 tsp ground cinnamon
- Salt and pepper, to taste
- 2 tbsp olive oil
- 2 oranges, sliced for garnish

For Orange-Pomegranate Preserves:
- 2 cups freshly squeezed orange juice
- 1 cup pomegranate juice
- Zest of one orange
- 1 cup granulated sugar
- 1/4 cup fresh lemon juice
- 1/2 cup pomegranate seeds

PROCEDURE

1 .In your small bowl, mix the cumin, coriander, and cinnamon. Season the Cornish hens with the spice mix, salt, and pepper.

2. .In your large skillet over medium-high heat, heat the olive oil. Brown the hens on all sides until golden brown. Set aside.

3. Prepare the Orange-Pomegranate Preserves by combining orange & pomegranate juice, zest, sugar, and lemon juice in your saucepan. Cook over medium heat until sugar dissolves.

4 .Add the hens and stir to coat them evenly. Cover and simmer within an hour or until hens are tender.

5. Fill your sterilized pint jars with equal amounts of hen pieces and Orange-Pomegranate Preserves, leaving a 1" headspace.

6 .Wipe the rims of your jars with a clean cloth, place lids plus rings on the jars, and tighten them finger-tight.

7 .Process jars in the pressure canner at 11 PSI for 75 minutes; adjust pressure for higher altitudes as needed.

8 .After elapsed processing time, turn off the heat, let the canner cool, and depressurize completely before removing the lid.

9 .Carefully remove jars and let them cool on a wire rack for 12-24 hours. Check lids for proper seals before storing.

Rabbit and Vegetable Medley

PREPARATION TIME

30 Minutes

COOKING TIME

75 Minutes

JAR SIZE

Quart Sized

YELD

7-8 Jars

PRESSURE

11 PSI

INGREDIENTS

- 4 pounds of rabbit meat, cut into pieces
- 4 cups baby carrots
- 4 cups fresh green beans, trimmed
- 4 cups diced new potatoes
- 2 cups chopped onions
- 1 cup chopped celery
- 2 cloves garlic, minced
- 1 tbsp salt
- 1 tbsp ground black pepper
- 8 cups chicken or rabbit broth

PROCEDURE

1. Place the rabbit meat, carrots, green beans, potatoes, onions, celery, garlic, salt, and pepper in your large stockpot.

2.. Pour the broth, then let it sit within a few minutes.

3. Pack the rabbit and vegetable mixture into sterilized quart jars, leaving 1" of headspace. Pour broth in each jar, maintaining 1" of headspace.

4. Wipe the rims of your jars with a clean cloth, place lids plus rings on the jars, and tighten them finger-tight.

5. Process jars in the pressure canner at 11 PSI for 75 minutes; adjust pressure for higher altitudes as needed.

6. After elapsed processing time, turn off the heat, let the canner cool, and depressurize completely before removing the lid.

7. Carefully remove jars and let them cool on a wire rack for 12-24 hours. Check lids for proper seals before storing.

Venison Stew

PREPARATION TIME

30 Minutes

COOKING TIME

75 Minutes

JAR SIZE

Pint Sized

YELD

6-8 Jars

PRESSURE

11 PSI

INGREDIENTS

- 3 pounds venison, cubed
- 4 cups potatoes, peeled and cubed
- 2 cups carrots, sliced
- 1 cup celery, chopped
- 1 large onion, diced
- 4 cloves garlic, minced
- 6 cups beef broth
- 2 cups tomato sauce
- 2 tbsp Worcestershire sauce
- 1 tsp dried thyme
- Salt & pepper, to taste

PROCEDURE

1. Mix the venison, potatoes, carrots, celery, onion, and garlic in your large bowl.

2. Combine the broth, tomato sauce, Worcestershire, thyme, salt, and pepper in your separate bowl.

3. Fill the sterilized pint jars with the venison mixture to about two-thirds full.

4. Pour the liquid mixture over the venison mixture in each jar, leaving a 1" headspace.

5. Wipe the rims of your jars with a clean cloth, place lids plus rings on the jars, and tighten them finger-tight.

6. Process jars in the pressure canner at 11 PSI for 75 minutes; adjust pressure for higher altitudes as needed.

7. After elapsed processing time, turn off the heat, let the canner cool, and depressurize completely before removing the lid.

8. Carefully remove jars and let them cool on a wire rack for 12-24 hours. Check lids for proper seals before storing.

SOUP, STOCK, AND BROTH

Green Lima Vegetable Soup

PREPARATION TIME

20 Minutes

COOKING TIME

60 Minutes

JAR SIZE

Pint Sized

YELD

7 Jars

PRESSURE

11 PSI

INGREDIENTS

- 4 cups sliced, peeled, cored tomatoes
- 3 cups ¾ inch chopped carrots
- 3 cups peeled & cubed potatoes
- 2 cups corn kernels, uncooked
- 2 cups green lima beans
- 1 cup sliced onions
- 1 cup 1-inch chopped celery
- Salt & pepper to taste
- 3 cups of water

PROCEDURE

1. In a medium saucepot, combine all the vegetables. Pour water and let it boil. Adjust to low heat, and cook for 5 minutes—season with pepper and salt.

2. Ladle hot veggie soup into each sterilized pint jar, leaving 1" headspace.

3. Wipe the rims of your jars with a clean cloth, place lids plus rings on the jars, and tighten them finger-tight.

4. Process jars in the pressure canner at 11 PSI for 55 minutes; adjust pressure for higher altitudes as needed.

5. After elapsed processing time, turn off the heat, let the canner cool, and depressurize completely before removing the lid.

6. Carefully remove jars and let them cool on a wire rack for 12-24 hours. Check lids for proper seals before storing.

Moroccan Sweet Potato Soup

PREPARATION TIME

30 Minutes

COOKING TIME

70 Minutes

JAR SIZE

Pint Sized

YELD

6 Jars

PRESSURE

11 PSI

INGREDIENTS

- 8 cups sweet potatoes, peeled & cut into ½-inch cubes
- 8 cups vegetable broth
- 4 cups water
- 1 medium sweet onion, diced
- 4 medium Roma tomatoes, diced
- 1½ cups fresh or frozen corn kernels
- 4 garlic cloves, minced
- 1 tbsp minced fresh ginger
- 2 tsp ground cumin
- 2 tsp ground coriander
- 1 tsp turmeric
- 1 tsp paprika
- 1 tsp ground cinnamon
- 1 tsp coarse sea salt
- ½ tsp ground black pepper

PROCEDURE

1. In a large stockpot, combine the sweet potatoes, broth, water, onion, tomatoes, corn, garlic, ginger, cumin, coriander, turmeric, paprika, cinnamon, salt, and pepper.

2. Let it boil over medium-high heat. Adjust to a simmer for 5 minutes, stirring often.

3. Ladle the hot soup into sterilized pint jars, leaving 1" of headspace.

4. Wipe the rims of your jars with a clean cloth, place lids plus rings on the jars, and tighten them finger-tight.

5. Process jars in the pressure canner at 11 PSI for 60 minutes; adjust pressure for higher altitudes as needed.

6. After processing time has elapsed, turn off the heat and allow the canner to cool and depressurize completely before removing the lid.

7. Carefully remove jars and let them cool on a wire rack for 12-24 hours. Check lids for proper seals before storing.

Chicken Tortilla Soup

PREPARATION TIME
30 Minutes

COOKING TIME
95 Minutes

JAR SIZE
Pint Sized

YELD
6 Jars

PRESSURE
11 PSI

INGREDIENTS

- 2 pounds shredded cooked chicken
- 1 large onion, chopped
- 3 cloves garlic, minced
- 1 tablespoon olive oil
- 1 (28 oz) can of crushed tomatoes
- 2 (15 oz each) cans of black beans, drained & rinsed
- 1 (15 oz) can of corn, drained & rinsed
- 1 (4 oz) can of diced green chilies, drained
- 6 cups chicken broth
- 1 tsp ground cumin
- 1 tsp chili powder
- Salt & pepper to taste

PROCEDURE

1. Heat the olive oil in your large skillet over medium heat. Add onions and garlic, and cook within 5 minutes until softened.

2. Combine cooked onions, garlic, chicken, broth, tomatoes, beans, corn, chilies, cumin, chili powder, salt, and pepper in a large pot.

3. Let it boil over high heat, and adjust to a simmer within 30 minutes.

4. Ladle the soup into the sterilized pint jars leaving about 1" of headspace.

5. Wipe the rims of your jars with a clean cloth, place lids plus rings on the jars, and tighten them finger-tight.

6. Process jars in the pressure canner at 11 PSI for 60 minutes; adjust pressure for higher altitudes as needed.

7. After elapsed processing time, turn off the heat, let the canner cool, and depressurize completely before removing the lid.

8. Carefully remove jars and let them cool on a wire rack for 12-24 hours. Check lids for proper seals before storing.

Chicken Chow Mein Soup

PREPARATION TIME
30 Minutes

COOKING TIME
95 Minutes

JAR SIZE
Quart Sized

YELD
6 Jars

PRESSURE
11 PSI

INGREDIENTS

- 2 pounds chicken breast, thinly sliced
- 3 tbsp vegetable oil
- 2 cloves garlic, minced
- 1 medium onion, finely chopped
- 2 cups cabbage, shredded
- 1 cup celery, sliced
- 1 cup bell peppers, thinly sliced (mixed colors)
- 2 cups bean sprouts
- 6 cups chicken broth
- 1/4 cup soy sauce
- 1/4 cup oyster sauce
- Salt & pepper, to taste

PROCEDURE

1. In your large frying pan over medium heat, heat the oil. Add garlic and onions, then cook until onions are translucent.

2. Add the chicken breast slices and cook until no longer pink.

3. Add cabbage, celery, peppers, and sprouts. Cook within 3 minutes to soften vegetables.

4. Warm the broth in a separate pot over medium-high heat, then season it with soy sauce and oyster sauce.

5. Pour chicken mixture into your pot with broth, mix well, and cook within 5 minutes. Adjust salt and pepper accordingly.

6. Ladle the hot soup into sterilized quart jars, leaving 1" headspace.

7. Wipe the rims of your jars with a clean cloth, place lids plus rings on the jars, and tighten them finger-tight.

8. Process jars in the pressure canner at 11 PSI for 80 minutes; adjust pressure for higher altitudes as needed.

9. After elapsed processing time, turn off the heat, let the canner cool, and depressurize completely before removing the lid.

10. Carefully remove jars and let them cool on a wire rack for 12-24 hours. Check lids for proper seals before storing.

French Onion Soup

PREPARATION TIME
30 Minutes

COOKING TIME
120 Minutes

JAR SIZE
Quart Sized

YELD
6 Jars

PRESSURE
11 PSI

INGREDIENTS

- 10 large onions, thinly sliced
- 2 tbsp olive oil
- 1 tbsp butter
- 6 cups beef or vegetable broth
- 3 cloves garlic, minced
- Salt & pepper, to taste
- 1 bay leaf
- 2 sprigs fresh thyme or ½ tsp dried thyme

PROCEDURE

1. Heat the olive oil and butter over medium heat in your large pot. Add the onions and cook within 20 minutes, stirring often until caramelized.

2. Add the garlic, salt, and pepper, then cook for another minute.

3. Pour in the broth, bay leaf, and thyme. Let it boil, adjust to low heat, and simmer within 40 minutes.

4. Fill each sterilized quart jar with the hot soup mixture leaving a ½" headspace.

5. Wipe the rims of your jars with a clean cloth, place lids plus rings on the jars, and tighten them finger-tight.

6. Process jars in the pressure canner at 11 PSI for 60 minutes; adjust pressure for higher altitudes as needed.

7. After elapsed processing time, turn off the heat, let the canner cool, and depressurize completely before removing the lid.

8. Carefully remove jars and let them cool on a wire rack for 12-24 hours. Check lids for proper seals before storing.

Carrot and Ginger Soup

PREPARATION TIME

30 Minutes

COOKING TIME

35 Minutes

JAR SIZE

Pint Sized

YELD

6 Jars

PRESSURE

11 PSI

INGREDIENTS

- 2 pounds carrots, peeled and chopped
- 1 large onion, chopped
- 2 cloves garlic, minced
- 1 tbsp fresh ginger, grated
- 4 cups vegetable broth
- 1 tsp ground coriander
- Salt & pepper, to taste

PROCEDURE

1. Combine the carrots, onion, garlic, ginger, and broth in your large pot. Let it boil over medium heat.

2. Adjust to low heat and simmer for 20-25 minutes until the carrots are tender.

3. Remove and let it cool slightly. Blend it using your immersion blender until smooth. Stir in coriander, salt, and pepper.

4. Prepare your pressure canner according to the manufacturer's instructions.

5. Fill your sterilized jars before with hot soup, leaving a 1" headspace.

6. Wipe the rims of your jars with a clean cloth, place lids plus rings on the jars, and tighten them finger-tight.

7. Process Jars in the pressure canner at 11 PSI for 15 minutes; adjust pressure for higher altitudes as needed.

8. After elapsed processing time, turn off the heat, let the canner cool, and depressurize completely before removing the lid.

9. Carefully remove jars and let them cool on a wire rack for 12-24 hours. Check lids for proper seals before storing.

Sausage and Bean Soup

PREPARATION TIME
30 Minutes

COOKING TIME
150 Minutes

JAR SIZE
Quart Sized

YELD
6 Jars

PRESSURE
11 PSI

INGREDIENTS

- 1-pound smoked sausage, sliced
- 2 cups dried mixed beans, soaked overnight & drained
- 8 cups chicken or vegetable broth
- 1 large onion, chopped
- 2 medium carrots, diced
- 1 celery stalk, diced
- 1 (14.5 oz) can of diced tomatoes with juice
- 2 cloves garlic, minced
- 1 tsp dried thyme
- Salt & pepper to taste

PROCEDURE

1. In your deep pot, brown the sausage within 5 minutes. Add onions, carrots, and celery, then sauté within 10 minutes until vegetables are tender.

2. Stir in beans, broth, tomatoes with juice, garlic, thyme, salt, and pepper.

3. Let it boil, and adjust to a simmer within 1 hour until beans are tender.

4. Fill sterilized quart jars with hot soup mixture, leaving a 1" headspace.

5. Wipe the rims of your jars with a clean cloth, place lids plus rings on the jars, and tighten them finger-tight.

6. Process jars in the pressure canner at 11 PSI for 75 minutes; adjust pressure for higher altitudes as needed.

7. After elapsed processing time, turn off the heat, let the canner cool, and depressurize completely before removing the lid.

8. Carefully remove jars and let them cool on a wire rack for 12-24 hours. Check lids for proper seals before storing.

Mexican Beef and Sweet Potato Soup

PREPARATION TIME
30 Minutes

COOKING TIME
75 Minutes

JAR SIZE
Pint Sized

YELD
6 Jars

PRESSURE
11 PSI

INGREDIENTS

- 1½ pounds of beef stew meat, cubed
- 3 cups of peeled and diced sweet potatoes
- 1 large onion, chopped
- 2 cloves garlic, minced
- 1 cup frozen corn kernels
- 1 (14.5 oz) can of diced tomatoes with green chilies
- 4 cups beef broth
- 2 tsp ground cumin
- 1 tsp chili powder
- Salt and pepper, to taste

PROCEDURE

1. In a large pan, brown the cubed beef on all sides over medium-high heat. Remove and set aside.

2. In the same pan, sauté the onions and garlic until translucent.

3. Add the browned beef, sweet potatoes, corn, diced tomatoes with green chilies, beef broth, cumin, chili powder, salt, and pepper.

4. Cook within 15 minutes until sweet potatoes are slightly tender but not mushy. Remove the pan.

5. Fill your sterilized pint jars evenly with hot soup mixture leaving 1" of headspace at the top.

6. Wipe the rims of your jars with a clean cloth, place lids plus rings on the jars, and tighten them finger-tight.

7. Process jars in the pressure canner at 11 PSI for 55 minutes; adjust pressure for higher altitudes as needed.

8. After elapsed processing time, turn off the heat, let the canner cool, and depressurize completely before removing the lid.

9. Carefully remove jars and let them cool on a wire rack for 12-24 hours. Check lids for proper seals before storing.

Split Pea Soup with Ham

PREPARATION TIME

20 Minutes

COOKING TIME

120 Minutes

JAR SIZE

Quart Sized

YELD

6 Jars

PRESSURE

11 PSI

INGREDIENTS

- 3 cups dried split peas, rinsed & drained
- 8 cups water
- 2 cups diced ham
- 1 large onion, chopped
- 2 medium carrots, peeled & diced
- 2 celery stalks, diced
- 2 cloves garlic, minced
- 1 bay leaf
- Salt & pepper, to taste

PROCEDURE

1. Add the split peas, water, ham, onion, carrots, celery, garlic, and bay leaf in your pressure cooker. Stir to combine.

2. Set the pressure cooker to high and lock the lid in place. Cook at high pressure within 1 hour or until the split peas are tender.

3. Allow the pressure to come down naturally. Carefully remove the lid and pressurize the canner. Stir well.

4. While hot, carefully ladle soup into sterilized quart jars, leaving 1" headspace.

5. Wipe the rims of your jars with a clean cloth, place lids plus rings on the jars, and tighten them finger-tight.

6. Process jars in the pressure canner at 11 PSI for 60 minutes; adjust pressure for higher altitudes as needed.

7. After elapsed processing time, turn off the heat, let the canner cool, and depressurize completely before removing the lid.

8. Carefully remove jars and let them cool on a wire rack for 12-24 hours. Check lids for proper seals before storing.

Lentil Soup with Carrots

PREPARATION TIME

20 Minutes

COOKING TIME

60 Minutes

JAR SIZE

Quart Sized

YELD

6 Jars

PRESSURE

10 PSI

INGREDIENTS

- 2 cups green or brown lentils, rinsed & drained
- 6 cups water
- 4 large carrots, peeled and diced
- 1 large onion, chopped
- 3 cloves garlic, minced
- 2 tsp ground cumin
- 1 tsp ground coriander
- Salt & pepper, to taste

PROCEDURE

1. In a large pot, combine the lentils and water. Let it boil over high heat, adjust to low heat and simmer within 15 minutes until lentils are tender.

2. Add the carrots, onion, garlic, cumin, coriander, salt, and pepper. Stir well to combine.

3. Let it simmer and cook for 15 minutes or until the vegetables are tender.

4. Carefully ladle the hot soup into clean, sterilized quart jars, leaving a 1" headspace.

5. Wipe the rims of your jars with a clean cloth, place lids plus rings on the jars, and tighten them finger-tight.

6. Process jars in the pressure canner at 10 PSI for 30 minutes; adjust pressure for higher altitudes as needed.

7. After elapsed processing time, turn off the heat, let the canner cool, and depressurize completely before removing the lid.

8. Carefully remove jars and let them cool on a wire rack for 12-24 hours. Check lids for proper seals before storing.

Pork and Sausage Stew

PREPARATION TIME
30 Minutes

COOKING TIME
135 Minutes

JAR SIZE
Quart Sized

YELD
6 Jars

PRESSURE
10 PSI

INGREDIENTS

- 2 pounds pork shoulder, cubed
- 1-pound smoked sausage, sliced
- 1 onion, chopped
- 3 cloves garlic, minced
- 2 carrots, chopped
- 2 celery stalks, chopped
- 1 bell pepper, chopped
- 4 cups beef broth
- 1 (14.5 oz) can of diced tomatoes
- 1 tsp paprika
- Salt & pepper, to taste

PROCEDURE

1. In your large pressure canner, sauté the onions and garlic until fragrant.

2. Add the pork shoulder and sausage and cook until brown on all sides. Stir in carrots, celery, bell pepper, tomatoes, paprika, salt, and pepper.

3. Pour the broth and stir everything thoroughly. Let it boil, and adjust to a simmer within 30 minutes.

4. Ladle the stew into cleaned and sterilized quart-sized jars, leaving 1" headspace in each jar.

5. Wipe the rims of your jars with a clean cloth, place lids plus rings on the jars, and tighten them finger-tight.

6. Process jars in the pressure canner at 11 PSI for 90 minutes; adjust pressure for higher altitudes as needed.

7. After elapsed processing time, turn off the heat, let the canner cool, and depressurize completely before removing the lid.

8. Carefully remove jars and let them cool on a wire rack for 12-24 hours. Check lids for proper seals before storing.

Chicken Stock

 PREPARATION TIME
20 Minutes

 COOKING TIME
5 Hours 30 Minutes

 JAR SIZE
Quart Sized

 YELD
6 Jars

 PRESSURE
10-11 PSI

INGREDIENTS

- 3 pounds of chicken bones and leftover carcass
- 1 large onion, quartered
- 2 carrots, chopped
- 2 celery stalks, chopped
- 1 head of garlic, halved horizontally
- Small bunch of fresh parsley
- 2 bay leaves
- 1 tsp black peppercorns
- Cold water to cover the ingredients (approximately 12 cups)

PROCEDURE

1. Place chicken bones, onion, carrots, celery, garlic, parsley, bay leaves, and peppercorns in a large stockpot.

2. Add enough cold water, and let it simmer over medium heat. Skim off any foam that forms above.

3. Adjust to low heat and simmer within 4 hours to develop flavors. Strain the stock through your fine-mesh strainer into a clean container. Discard solids.

4. Let it cool at room temperature within an hour before placing it in the refrigerator for further cooling and overnight storage.

5. The next day, remove the chilled stock and skim off any fat layer that has formed on its surface. Reheat the stock but do not boil.

6. Fill your sterilized quart jars with hot chicken stock leaving about 1" of headspace.

7. Wipe the rims of your jars with a clean cloth, place lids plus rings on the jars, and tighten them finger-tight.

8. Process jars in the pressure canner at 10-11 PSI for 90 minutes; adjust pressure for higher altitudes as needed.

9. After processing time has elapsed, turn off the heat and allow the canner to cool and depressurize completely before removing the lid.

10. Carefully remove jars and let them cool on a wire rack for 12-24 hours. Check lids for proper seals before storing.

Fish Stock

PREPARATION TIME	COOKING TIME	JAR SIZE	YELD	PRESSURE
30 Minutes	75 Minutes	Quart Sized	6 Jars	10 PSI

INGREDIENTS

- 6 pounds fish bones and heads, gills removed
- 2 onions, roughly chopped
- 2 carrots, roughly chopped
- 2 celery stalks, roughly chopped
- 1 leek, cleaned & roughly chopped
- 12 cups cold water
- 3 bay leaves
- A handful of fresh parsley stems
- A few sprigs of fresh thyme

PROCEDURE

1. Combine fish bones & heads, onions, carrots, celery, leek, cold water, bay leaves, parsley stems, and thyme in your large stockpot.

2. Let it simmer over medium heat. Skim off any foam that appears above.

3. Simmer within 45 minutes on low heat until the stock has a rich aroma and flavor.

4. Strain the fish stock through your fine-mesh sieve lined with cheesecloth into a large pot or bowl. Discard the solids.

5. Pour the strained stock into clean and sterilized quart-sized jars, leaving 1" headspace at the top of each jar.

6. Wipe the rims of your jars with a clean cloth, place lids plus rings on the jars, and tighten them finger-tight.

7. Process jars in the pressure canner at 10 PSI for 90 minutes; adjust pressure for higher altitudes as needed.

8. After elapsed processing time, turn off the heat, let the canner cool, and depressurize completely before removing the lid.

9. Carefully remove jars and let them cool on a wire rack for 12-24 hours. Check lids for proper seals before storing.

Shellfish Stock

PREPARATION TIME

30 Minutes

COOKING TIME

95 Minutes

JAR SIZE

Pint Sized

YELD

6 Jars

PRESSURE

10 PSI

INGREDIENTS

- 2 pounds shellfish shells (shrimp, crab, or lobster)
- 1 large onion, chopped
- 2 carrots, chopped
- 2 celery stalks, chopped
- 1 bay leaf
- 1 tsp black peppercorns
- 4 sprigs of fresh thyme
- 4 cloves garlic, minced
- 8 cups cold water

PROCEDURE

1. In your large stockpot, add shellfish shells and cook over medium heat within 5 minutes until they turn pink.

2. Add onion, carrots, celery, bay leaf, peppercorns, thyme, garlic, and cold water.

3. Let it boil, and simmer uncovered within 1 hour. Strain the stock through your fine mesh strainer into a clean pot or container. Discard solids.

4. Fill sterilized jars with hot shellfish stock, leaving a 1" headspace.

5. Wipe the rims of your jars with a clean cloth, place lids plus rings on the jars, and tighten them finger-tight.

6. Process jars in the pressure canner at 10 PSI for 90 minutes; adjust pressure for higher altitudes as needed.

7. After elapsed processing time, turn off the heat, let the canner cool, and depressurize completely before removing the lid.

8. Carefully remove jars and let them cool on a wire rack for 12-24 hours. Check lids for proper seals before storing.

Turkey Bone Broth

PREPARATION TIME
30 Minutes

COOKING TIME
115 Minutes

JAR SIZE
Quart Sized

YELD
4 Jars

PRESSURE
11 PSI

INGREDIENTS

- Turkey bones (from one cooked turkey)
- 2 large carrots, sliced
- 2 celery stalks, sliced
- 1 large onion, quartered
- 4 cloves of garlic, crushed
- 1 tbsp apple cider vinegar
- Salt & pepper to taste
- Water, as needed

PROCEDURE

1. Place the turkey bones in the pressure canner. Add carrots, celery, onion, and garlic. Pour in water until everything is covered.

2. Add apple cider vinegar, salt, and pepper. Seal the pressure canner with its lid and heat on medium-high heat.

3. When the canner achieves a steady steam flow, attach the pressure regulator to the vent pipe and adjust to 11 PSI.

4. Cook under pressure for 1 hour and 30 minutes. After cooking, turn off the heat and allow the pressure to drop naturally in the canner before opening.

5. Strain your broth through your fine mesh sieve into a bowl, removing solids.

6. Pour strained broth into sterilized quart jars, leaving a 1" headspace at each jar's top.

7. Wipe the rims of your jars with a clean cloth, place lids plus rings on the jars, and tighten them finger-tight.

8. Process jars in the pressure canner at 11 PSI for 25 minutes; adjust pressure for higher altitudes as needed.

9. After elapsed processing time, turn off the heat, let the canner cool, and depressurize completely before removing the lid.

10. Carefully remove jars and let them cool on a wire rack for 12-24 hours. Check lids for proper seals before storing.

Mushroom Broth

PREPARATION TIME

30 Minutes

COOKING TIME

92 Minutes

JAR SIZE

Pint Sized

YELD

6 Jars

PRESSURE

11 PSI

INGREDIENTS

- 3 pounds fresh mushrooms, sliced
- 1 large onion, chopped
- 4 cloves of garlic, minced
- 10 cups water
- 2 tbsp olive oil
- Salt & pepper to taste

PROCEDURE

1. In your large pot, heat the olive oil over medium heat. Add the onions and cook within 5 minutes until they become translucent.

2. Add the garlic and cook within 2 minutes. Add the mushrooms and cook within 10 minutes until they start to brown—season with salt and pepper.

3. Pour the water and let it boil. Adjust to low heat, cover, and simmer within 1 hour.

4. Strain the broth through your fine-mesh sieve into a clean container, discarding the solids.

5. Ladle hot mushroom broth into your sterilized pint jar, leaving a 1" headspace at the top.

6. Wlpe the rims of your jars with a clean cloth, place lids plus rings on the jars, and tighten them finger-tight.

7. Process jars in the pressure canner at 11 PSI for 75 minutes; adjust pressure for higher altitudes as needed.

8. After elapsed processing time, turn off the heat, let the canner cool, and depressurize completely before removing the lid.

9. Carefully remove jars and let them cool on a wire rack for 12-24 hours. Check lids for proper seals before storing.

Beef Broth

PREPARATION TIME
20 Minutes

COOKING TIME
175 Minutes

JAR SIZE
Quart Sized

YELD
6-7 Jars

PRESSURE
11 PSI

INGREDIENTS

- 5 pounds of beef bones (with meat still attached)
- 1 large onion, roughly chopped
- 2 carrots, roughly chopped
- 2 celery stalks, roughly chopped
- 2 tbsp tomato paste
- 2 cloves garlic, minced
- 10 cups water
- 1/4 cup apple cider vinegar
- Salt & pepper to taste

PROCEDURE

1. Preheat oven to 400°F. Place beef bones on your baking sheet and roast for 20 minutes.

2. In a large stockpot, sauté onions, carrots, and celery until softened. Add roasted beef bones and tomato paste to the pot.

3. Stir in garlic and cook for another minute. Add water and apple cider vinegar.

4. Let it boil, adjust to low heat, and simmer within 1 hour—season with salt and pepper.

5. Strain the broth through your fine-mesh sieve into a clean pot, discarding the solid.

6. Ladle hot broth into your sterilized quart jars, leaving 1" headspace at the top of each jar.

7. Wipe the rims of your jars with a clean cloth, place lids plus rings on the jars, and tighten them finger-tight.

8. Process jars in the pressure canner at 11 PSI for 90 minutes; adjust pressure for higher altitudes as needed.

9. After elapsed processing time, turn off the heat, let the canner cool, and depressurize completely before removing the lid.

10. Carefully remove jars and let them cool on a wire rack for 12-24 hours. Check lids for proper seals before storing.

Vegetable Broth

PREPARATION TIME

30 Minutes

COOKING TIME

85 Minutes

JAR SIZE

Quart Sized

YELD

6 Jars

PRESSURE

11 PSI

INGREDIENTS

- 3 large carrots, coarsely chopped
- 2 medium onions, coarsely chopped
- 3 celery stalks, coarsely chopped
- 1 cup mushrooms, sliced
- 2 cups spinach or kale leaves, torn
- 8 cups water
- 2 cloves garlic, minced
- 1 bay leaf
- 1 bunch parsley or cilantro, chopped
- Salt & pepper to taste

PROCEDURE

1. Combine the carrots, onions, celery, mushrooms, spinach, garlic, and bay leaf in your large stockpot. Pour in the water.

2. Let it boil over high heat. Adjust to low heat and simmer within 1 hour.

3. Strain the vegetable mixture into a clean pot, removing the vegetables. Add salt and pepper.

4. Fill your sterilized quart jars with hot vegetable broth, leaving a 1" headspace at the top of each jar.

5. Wipe the rims of your jars with a clean cloth, place lids plus rings on the jars, and tighten them finger-tight.

6. Process jars in the pressure canner at 11 PSI for 25 minutes; adjust pressure for higher altitudes as needed.

7. After elapsed processing time, turn off the heat, let the canner cool, and depressurize completely before removing the lid.

8. Carefully remove jars and let them cool on a wire rack for 12-24 hours. Check lids for proper seals before storing.

SAUCE
RECIPES

Caramel Sauce

PREPARATION TIME

20 Minutes

COOKING TIME

35 Minutes

JAR SIZE

Pint Sized

YELD

3 Jars

PRESSURE

10 PSI

INGREDIENTS

- 2 cups granulated sugar
- 1/2 cup water
- 1/2 cup unsalted butter, cubed
- 1 cup heavy cream
- 1 tsp vanilla extract
- 1/4 tsp salt

PROCEDURE

1. Combine sugar and water in your saucepan over medium heat until the sugar has dissolved.

2. Continue to cook without stirring, allowing the mixture to caramelize and turn golden brown.

3. Meanwhile, heat the heavy cream in a separate saucepan until it's warm but not boiling.

4. Remove the caramel saucepan and add the cubed butter, stirring until melted. Gradually pour in heavy cream while stirring until smooth.

5. Add salt and vanilla, stirring to combine. Allow the caramel sauce to cool slightly.

6. Fill sterilized jars with caramel sauce, leaving a ¼" headspace at the top of each jar.

7. Wipe the rims of your jars with a clean cloth, place lids plus rings on the jars, and tighten them finger-tight.

8. Process jars in the pressure canner at 10 PSI for 10 minutes; adjust pressure for higher altitudes as needed.

9. After elapsed processing time, turn off the heat, let the canner cool, and depressurize completely before removing the lid.

10. Carefully remove jars and let them cool on a wire rack for 12-24 hours. Check lids for proper seals before storing.

Chili Sauce

PREPARATION TIME
30 Minutes

COOKING TIME
125 Minutes

JAR SIZE
Pint Sized

YELD
8 Jars

PRESSURE
11 PSI

INGREDIENTS

- 10 cups tomatoes, peeled & chopped
- 2 cups onions, chopped
- 2 cups bell peppers, chopped
- 1 cup jalapeño peppers, seeded & finely chopped
- 2 cups apple cider vinegar
- 1 cup brown sugar
- 2 tsp salt
- 1 tsp black pepper
- 1 tsp ground cumin

PROCEDURE

1. Combine tomatoes, onions, peppers, jalapeño, apple cider, sugar, salt, black pepper, and cumin in your large pot.

2. Let it boil over medium-high heat. Adjust to low heat and simmer within 45 minutes or until thickened, stirring often.

3. Ladle the hot chili sauce into the sterilized pint jars leaving a ½" headspace.

4. Wipe the rims of your jars with a clean cloth, place lids plus rings on the jars, and tighten them finger-tight.

5. Process jars in the pressure canner at 11 PSI for 60 minutes; adjust pressure for higher altitudes as needed.

6. After elapsed processing time, turn off the heat, let the canner cool, and depressurize completely before removing the lid.

7. Carefully remove jars and let them cool on a wire rack for 12-24 hours. Check lids for proper seals before storing.

Tomato Sauce

PREPARATION TIME

30 Minutes

COOKING TIME

35 Minutes

JAR SIZE

Pint Sized

YELD

8 Jars

PRESSURE

11 PSI

INGREDIENTS

- 10 pounds fresh tomatoes, washed, cored & cut into quarters
- 2 cups chopped onions
- 4 cloves of garlic, minced
- 1/4 cup olive oil
- 2 tsp salt
- 1 tsp ground black pepper
- 1 tsp dried basil
- 1 tsp dried oregano

PROCEDURE

1. In your large saucepan, heat olive oil over medium heat. Add onions and garlic and sauté within 5 minutes until softened.

2. Add the tomatoes, salt, pepper, basil, and oregano. Let it boil, and simmer within 10 minutes.

3. Blend the sauce using your immersion blender until smooth.

4. Pour hot tomato sauce into your sterilized pint jar, leaving a ½" headspace from the top of the jar.

5. Wipe the rims of your jars with a clean cloth, place lids plus rings on the jars, and tighten them finger-tight.

6. Process jars in the pressure canner at 11 PSI for 20 minutes; adjust pressure for higher altitudes as needed.

7. After elapsed processing time, turn off the heat, let the canner cool, and depressurize completely before removing the lid.

8. Carefully remove jars and let them cool on a wire rack for 12-24 hours. Check lids for proper seals before storing.

Spaghetti Sauce

PREPARATION TIME
30 Minutes

COOKING TIME
125 Minutes

JAR SIZE
Quart Sized

YELD
7 Jars

PRESSURE
11 PSI

INGREDIENTS

- 12 cups fresh tomatoes, peeled & chopped
- 2 cups onions, chopped
- 1 cup green bell pepper, chopped
- 4 cloves garlic, minced
- 2 tbsp olive oil
- 3 cups tomato paste
- 1/4 cup sugar
- 1 tbsp salt
- 4 tsp dried basil leaves
- 4 tsp dried oregano leaves
- 2 tsp black pepper

PROCEDURE

1. Heat the olive oil in your large pot over medium heat. Add onions, bell pepper, and garlic. Cook within 5 minutes until softened.

2. Stir in tomatoes and let it boil. Adjust to a simmer, uncovered, within 20 minutes or until tomatoes are softened.

3. Add tomato paste, sugar, salt, basil, oregano, plus pepper. Stir well. Let it boil then and simmer within 30 minutes, stirring often.

4. Ladle the hot spaghetti sauce into the sterilized quart jars, leaving a 1" headspace at the top.

5. Wipe the rims of your jars with a clean cloth, place lids plus rings on the jars, and tighten them finger-tight.

6. Process jars in the pressure canner at 11 PSI for 75 minutes; adjust pressure for higher altitudes as needed.

7. After elapsed processing time, turn off the heat, let the canner cool, and depressurize completely before removing the lid.

8. Carefully remove jars and let them cool on a wire rack for 12-24 hours. Check lids for proper seals before storing.

Teriyaki Sauce

PREPARATION TIME

30 Minutes

COOKING TIME

35 Minutes

JAR SIZE

Half Pint Sized

YELD

6 Jars

PRESSURE

11 PSI

INGREDIENTS

- 1 cup soy sauce
- 1/2 cup water
- 1/2 cup honey
- 1/4 cup rice vinegar
- 1 tbsp finely grated ginger
- 2 cloves garlic, minced
- 1 tsp sesame oil

PROCEDURE

1. Combine soy sauce, water, honey, rice vinegar, ginger, garlic, and sesame oil in your medium saucepan.

2. Let it boil over medium-high heat, and simmer within 15 minutes or until slightly thickened.

3. Carefully ladle the hot teriyaki sauce into the sterilized jars, leaving a ¼" headspace.

4. Wipe the jar rims clean with a damp cloth and secure the lids with screw bands until fingertip tight.

5. Wipe the rims of your jars with a clean cloth, place lids plus rings on the jars, and tighten them finger-tight.

6. Process jars in the pressure canner at 11 PSI for 20 minutes; adjust pressure for higher altitudes as needed.

7. After elapsed processing time, turn off the heat, let the canner cool, and depressurize completely before removing the lid.

8. Carefully remove jars and let them cool on a wire rack for 12-24 hours. Check lids for proper seals before storing.

BBQ Sauce

PREPARATION TIME

20 Minutes

COOKING TIME

50 Minutes

JAR SIZE

Pint Sized

YELD

10 Jars

PRESSURE

10 PSI

INGREDIENTS

- 6 cups ketchup
- 3 cups brown sugar
- 3 cups white vinegar
- 1 1/2 cups Worcestershire sauce
- 1 1/2 cups soy sauce
- 9 cloves garlic, minced
- 6 tbsp onion powder
- 6 tbsp black pepper
- 3 tbsp smoked paprika

PROCEDURE

1. In your large pot, mix all the ingredients until the sugar dissolves completely.

2. Let it simmer over medium heat and cook within 30 minutes, stirring often.

3. Carefully ladle it into the sterilized pint jars, leaving a ½" headspace at the top of each jar.

4. Wipe the rims of your jars with a clean cloth, place lids plus rings on the jars, and tighten them finger-tight.

5. Process jars in the pressure canner at 11 PSI for 20 minutes; adjust pressure for higher altitudes as needed.

6. After elapsed processing time, turn off the heat, let the canner cool, and depressurize completely before removing the lid.

7. Carefully remove jars and let them cool on a wire rack for 12-24 hours. Check lids for proper seals before storing.

Greek Tzatziki Sauce

PREPARATION TIME

20 Minutes

COOKING TIME

10 Minutes

JAR SIZE

Half Pint Sized

YELD

8 Jars

PRESSURE

11 PSI

INGREDIENTS

- 4 cups Greek yogurt
- 2 large cucumbers, peeled, seeded, & grated
- 4 cloves garlic, minced
- 1/3 cup fresh dill, chopped
- 1/4 cup fresh mint leaves, chopped
- Juice of 1 lemon
- Salt & pepper to taste

PROCEDURE

1. Combine the yogurt, grated cucumber, minced garlic, dill, mint leaves, lemon juice, salt, and pepper in a large bowl.

2. Fill the jars evenly with the tzatziki sauce mixture, leaving about a ½" headspace at the top.

3. Wipe the rims of your jars with a clean cloth, place lids plus rings on the jars, and tighten them finger-tight.

4. Process jars in the pressure canner at 11 PSI for 10 minutes; adjust pressure for higher altitudes as needed.

5. After elapsed processing time, turn off the heat, let the canner cool, and depressurize completely before removing the lid.

6. Carefully remove jars and let them cool on a wire rack for 12-24 hours. Check lids for proper seals before storing.

Bolognese Sauce

PREPARATION TIME
30 Minutes

COOKING TIME
130 Minutes

JAR SIZE
Pint Sized

YELD
6-8 Jars

PRESSURE
11 PSI

INGREDIENTS

- 2 pounds of ground beef
- 2 onions, finely chopped
- 4 cloves garlic, minced
- 2 carrots, peeled and diced
- 2 celery stalks, diced
- 1 cup red wine
- 1 (28 oz) can of crushed tomatoes
- 1 (6 oz) can of tomato paste
- 2 cups beef broth
- 2 tsp dried basil
- 2 tsp dried oregano
- Salt & pepper, to taste

PROCEDURE

1. In a pressure cooker, brown the ground beef on medium-high heat. Remove and set aside.

2. Sauté onions, garlic, carrots, and celery in the same pressure cooker until soft.

3. Add the ground beef back into your pressure cooker along with the red wine. Allow it to simmer within a couple of minutes.

4. Stir in crushed tomatoes, tomato paste, broth, basil, oregano, salt, and pepper.

5. Lock the pressure cooker lid and set it to high pressure. Cook for 45 minutes.

6. Release the pressure from your cooker according to the manufacturer's instructions.

7. Carefully transfer the hot Bolognese sauce into your sterilized jars, leaving a ½" headspace.

8. Wipe the rims of your jars with a clean cloth, place lids plus rings on the jars, and tighten them finger-tight.

9. Process jars in the pressure canner at 11 PSI for 75 minutes; adjust pressure for higher altitudes as needed.

10. After elapsed processing time, turn off the heat, let the canner cool, and depressurize completely before removing the lid.

11. Carefully remove jars and let them cool on a wire rack for 12-24 hours. Check lids for proper seals before storing.

COOKING CONVERSION CHART

Volume Equivalents (Liquid)

US STANDARD	US STANDARD (OUNCES)	METRIC (APPROXIMATE)
2 tablespoons	1 fl. oz.	30 mL
¼ cup	2 fl. oz.	60 mL
½ cup	4 fl. oz.	120 mL
1 cup	8 fl. oz.	240 mL
1½ cups	12 fl. oz.	355 mL
2 cups or 1 pint	16 fl. oz.	475 mL
4 cups or 1 quart	32 fl. oz.	1 L
1 gallon	128 fl. oz.	4 L

Volume Equivalents (Dry)

US STANDARD	METRIC (APPROXIMATE)
⅛ teaspoon	0.5 mL
¼ teaspoon	1 mL
½ teaspoon	2 mL
¾ teaspoon	4 mL
1 teaspoon	5 mL
1 tablespoon	15 mL
¼ cup	59 mL
⅓ cup	79 mL
½ cup	118 mL
⅔ cup	156 mL
¾ cup	177 mL
1 cup	235 mL
2 cups or 1 pint	475 mL
3 cups	700 mL
4 cups or 1 quart	1 L
½ gallon	2 L
1 gallon	4 L

Oven Temperatures

FAHRENHEIT (F)	CELSIUS (C) (APPROXIMATE)
250	120
300	150
325	165
350	180
375	190
400	200
425	220
450	230

Weight Equivalents

US STANDARD	METRIC (APPROXIMATE)
½ ounce	15 g
1 ounce	30 g
2 ounces	60 g
4 ounces	115 g
8 ounces	225 g
12 ounces	340 g
16 ounces or 1 pound	455 g

STATE	CAPITAL	ALTITUDE (FT)	PRESSURE INCREASE (PSI)
AL	Montgomery	195	0
AK	Juneau	0	0
AZ	Phoenix	1,086	2
AR	Little Rock	335	0
CA	Sacramento	30	0
CO	Denver	5,280	4
CT	Hartford	30	0
DE	Dover	60	0
FL	Tallahassee	60	0
GA	Atlanta	1,050	2
HI	Honolulu	19	0
ID	Boise	2,842	3
IL	Springfield	600	0
IN	Indianapolis	650	0
IA	Des Moines	950	0
KS	Topeka	1,025	2
KY	Frankfort	700	0
LA	Baton Rouge	10	0
ME	Augusta	85	0
MD	Annapolis	30	0
MA	Boston	20	0
MI	Lansing	600	0
MN	St. Paul	830	0
MS	Jackson	297	0
MO	Jefferson City	650	0
MT	Helena	3,400	3

STATE	CAPITAL	ALTITUDE (FT)	PRESSURE INCREASE (PSI)
NE	Lincoln	1,170	2
NV	Carson City	4,500	4
NH	Concord	325	0
NJ	Trenton	60	0
NM	Santa Fe	5,312	4
NY	Albany	365	0
NC	Raleigh	870	0
ND	Bismarck	900	0
OH	Columbus	850	0
OK	Oklahoma City	1,201	2
OR	Salem	50	0
PA	Harrisburg	370	0
RI	Providence	40	0
SC	Columbia	350	0
SD	Pierre	1,430	2
TN	Nashville	580	0
TX	Austin	489	0
UT	Salt Lake City	4,330	4
VT	Montpelier	380	0
VA	Richmond	30	0
WA	Olympia	350	0
WV	Charleston	975	0
WI	Madison	860	0
WY	Cheyenne	6,700	5

BONUS

FERMENTING

Fermentation, as a method of preserving food, has been utilized for ages, and its practices have successfully proven their effectiveness throughout history. Fermented foods provide a completely natural way of preserving freshness while maintaining the flavors of vegetables over extended periods, without the use of chemical additives or blanching procedures.

Jar fermentation has been adopted in almost every household, and individuals who enjoy cooking are now more aware than ever of its growing popularity. This method offers guaranteed safety measures during consumption, even after preservation. Its numerous advantageous aspects make it a worthwhile choice.

Fermenting vegetables involves nourishing microorganisms, such as lactobacilli, that naturally break down sugars present on their surfaces. This process releases lactic acids, resulting in lowered pH levels within the jars. The acidic environment created by fermentation discourages microbial survival, making the fermented food safe to eat.

Another advantage associated with lactic acids released during fermentation is the creation of an enjoyable, slightly tangy flavor and a crispy texture that most people find irresistible. To achieve optimal results, experts recommend following specific guidelines for fermenting vegetables, such as using fresh vegetables from local or organic sources, meticulously cleaning them, not leaving out any damaged parts, and using a clean, tightly sealed glass container.

The container creates an oxygen-free environment that promotes ideal bacterial growth, enabling successful fermentation results.

FOODS SUITABLE FOR FERMENTATION:
1. Vegetables (e.g., pickles, carrots, cabbage, peppers)
2. Legumes (e.g., beans, lentils)
3. Grains (e.g., wheat for yeast production)
4. Condiments (e.g., soy sauce, miso)
5. Beverages (e.g., kombucha, kefir)

FOODS NOT SUITABLE FOR FERMENTATION:
1. **Fresh meat:** Home fermentation is not suitable for preserving fresh meat. Fermentation may not be sufficient to prevent the proliferation of harmful bacteria.

2. **Fresh fish:** Similar to fresh meat, fresh fish is not suitable for home fermentation. Proper fish preservation requires specific methods to ensure food safety.

3. **Fresh milk:** Fresh milk is not suitable for home fermentation. However, fresh milk can be used as a base to produce yogurt or kefir by adding specific bacterial cultures.

4. **Fresh fruit:** Home fermentation is not commonly used for preserving fresh fruit. However, certain fruit varieties can be used as ingredients in specific fermentations, such as using apples for cider production.

5. **High-sugar foods:** Foods with a high sugar content, such as candies, chocolates, or desserts in general, are not suitable for home fermentation. Fermentation requires a high concentration of fermentable sugars, which may result in undesirable outcomes in this case.

6. **Foods with chemical preservatives:** Foods that contain added chemical preservatives, such as industrially packaged products, may not be suitable for home fermentation. Chemical preservatives can negatively affect fermentation or the final outcome.

NECESSARY MATERIALS:

1. **Fresh vegetables:** Choose high-quality fresh vegetables, such as cabbage, carrots, cucumbers, or radishes. Ensure they are clean and free from imperfections.

2. **Glass jars:** Use clean glass jars with airtight lids. Glass jars allow you to observe the fermentation process and safely store the vegetables.

3. **Salt:** Use non-iodized sea salt or fermentation salt to regulate the fermentation process and preserve the vegetables.

4. **Spices and flavorings:** Add spices and flavorings to enhance the taste of the fermented vegetables. You can use spices like mustard seeds, whole peppercorns, chili, garlic, or ginger.

5. **Fermentation weight:** Use a specially designed weight for fermentation to keep the vegetables submerged in water during the fermentation process.

6. **Cabbage leaves:** Cabbage leaves can be used to cover the vegetables inside the jar and keep them submerged in water during fermentation.

7. **Sharp knife:** A sharp knife will allow you to cut the vegetables into desired pieces or slices.

8. **Cutting board:** Use a clean and sturdy cutting board to cut the vegetables without damaging the work surfaces.

9. **Bowl:** Use a bowl to mix the vegetables with salt and spices before placing them in the jar.

10. **Permanent marker:** Use a permanent marker to label the jars with the type of vegetable and the start date of fermentation.

Make sure you have these materials on hand to facilitate the safe and high-quality vegetable fermentation process in jars.

PROCEDURE

1. **Vegetable preparation:**
   - Thoroughly wash the fresh vegetables and remove any unwanted parts.
   - Cut the vegetables into desired pieces or slices.

2. **Brine preparation:**
   - In a bowl, mix filtered water and non-iodized sea salt to create a brine solution. Ensure that the salt is completely dissolved.

3. **Filling the jars:**
   - Place the cut ingredients inside clean and sterilized glass jars.
   - Pour the brine solution into the jar, making sure the vegetables are completely submerged in the liquid. Leave some headspace at the top of the jar to allow for fermentation.

4. **Weight and cover:**
   - Place a clean cabbage leaf on top of the vegetables to keep them submerged during fermentation.
   - Use a fermentation weight to gently press the vegetables down, ensuring they remain under the liquid.

5. **Jar sealing:**
   - Seal the jar with the airtight lid, ensuring it is tightly closed.

6. **Fermentation:**
   - Place the jars in a room temperature location away from direct sunlight.
   - Let the vegetables ferment for 1-2 weeks, periodically checking the fermentation process. Bubbles will form, and the flavor of the vegetables will develop during this time.

7. **Monitoring the fermentation process:**
   - Check the jar daily to ensure the vegetables stay submerged and no mold or signs of spoilage form. If necessary, remove any unwanted formations from the surface.

8. **Fermentation completion:**
   - Once the desired level of fermentation is reached, seal the jar tightly and transfer it to the refrigerator to further slow down the fermentation process.

9. **Storage and consumption:**
   - Store the fermented vegetables in the refrigerator and consume them within a reasonable period to maintain freshness and flavor.

During the fermentation process, it is important to follow proper hygiene and food safety procedures. Ensure that utensils and jars are properly cleaned and sterilized, and wash hands thoroughly before handling the ingredients.

Napa Cabbage Kimchi

PREPARATION TIME
1 HOUR

FERMENTATION
3-5 DAYS

INGREDIENTS

- 1 medium Napa cabbage
- 2 carrots
- 4 spring onions
- 4 cloves of garlic
- 1 tablespoon grated fresh ginger
- 2 tablespoons fish sauce
- 1 tablespoon chili powder
- 1 teaspoon sugar
- Sea salt to taste

PROCEDURE

1. Cut the Napa cabbage in half lengthwise and remove the core. Cut the cabbage into wide strips.
2. Peel and cut the carrots into sticks.
3. Slice the spring onions thinly.
4. In a large bowl, mix together the cabbage, carrots, spring onions, garlic, ginger, fish sauce, chili powder, and sugar.
5. Add sea salt to taste and mix well to release the water from the vegetables.
6. Transfer the mixture into the fermentation tray of a clean jar and press it down firmly to cover the vegetables with the liquid that has been formed.
7. Seal the jar tightly and let it ferment at room temperature for 3-5 days.
8. Transfer the kimchi to the refrigerator and let it ferment for at least another two weeks before consuming.

Red Cabbage Curtido

PREPARATION TIME
45 MINUTES

FERMENTATION
2-3 DAYS

INGREDIENTS

- 1 medium red cabbage
- 2 carrots
- 1 red onion
- 1 green apple
- Juice of 2 limes
- 2 tablespoons apple cider vinegar
- 1 teaspoon sugar
- 1 teaspoon cumin seeds
- Sea salt to taste

PROCEDURE

1. Thinly slice the red cabbage, grate the carrots, thinly slice the red onion, and julienne the green apple.
2. In a large bowl, mix together the red cabbage, carrots, red onion, green apple, lime juice, apple cider vinegar, sugar, cumin seeds, and salt.
3. Massage the mixture well to release the water from the vegetables.
4. Transfer the mixture into the fermentation tray of a clean jar and press it down firmly to cover the vegetables with the liquid that has been formed.
5. Seal the jar tightly and let it ferment at room temperature for 2-3 days.
6. Transfer the curtido to the refrigerator and let it ferment for at least another two weeks before consuming.

Beet Sauerbraten

PREPARATION TIME
30 MINUTES

FERMENTATION
1-2 WEEKS

INGREDIENTS

- 4 medium beets
- 2 tablespoons sea salt
- 1 tablespoon cumin seeds
- 1 tablespoon coriander seeds
- 4 whole cloves
- 4 juniper berries
- 2 bay leaves
- 1 tablespoon apple cider vinegar
- 2 cups water

PROCEDURE

1. Peel and thinly slice the beets.

2. In a bowl, mix together sea salt, cumin seeds, coriander seeds, cloves, juniper berries, and bay leaves.

3. Layer beets on the bottom of a clean fermentation jar and sprinkle with some of the spice mixture.

4. Continue layering beets and spices until the jar is filled.

5. Mix apple cider vinegar with water and pour the mixture into the jar, completely covering the beets.

6. Seal the jar tightly and let it ferment at room temperature for 1-2 weeks.

7. Transfer the beet sauerbraten to the refrigerator and let it ferment for at least another two weeks before consuming.

Daikon Radish Kimchi

PREPARATION TIME
1 HOUR

FERMENTATION
3-5 DAYS

INGREDIENTS

- 2 medium daikon radishes
- 2 tablespoons sea salt
- 2 tablespoons chili powder
- 2 cloves of garlic, minced
- 1 tablespoon grated fresh ginger
- 2 spring onions, sliced
- 1 tablespoon sugar

PROCEDURE

1. Peel the daikon radishes and cut them into thin sticks.

2. In a bowl, mix the daikon radishes with sea salt and let them sit for 30 minutes to release the water.

3. Drain the released water and add chili powder, minced garlic, grated ginger, spring onions, and sugar. Mix well.

4. Transfer the mixture to the fermentation tray of a clean jar and press it down firmly to cover the daikon radishes with the liquid that has been formed.

5. Seal the jar tightly and let it ferment at room temperature for 3-5 days.

6. Transfer the daikon radish kimchi to the refrigerator and let it ferment for at least another two weeks before consuming.

Fermented Tomato Sauce

PREPARATION TIME
30 MINUTES

FERMENTATION
3-5 DAYS

INGREDIENTS

- 2.2 lbs ripe tomatoes
- 2 tablespoons kosher salt
- 2 cloves of garlic, minced
- 1 small onion, chopped
- 1 red chili pepper, minced (optional)
- 1 teaspoon sugar
- 1 teaspoon apple cider vinegar
- 2 cups chlorine-free water

PROCEDURE

1. Wash the tomatoes and remove the stem. Cut them into small pieces and place them in a bowl.

2. Add kosher salt to the tomatoes and mix well to distribute it evenly. Let it sit for 15 minutes to release the juice from the tomatoes.

3. Add minced garlic, chopped onion, and minced red chili pepper (if desired) to the tomatoes. Mix well.

4. Transfer the tomato mixture to a clean and sterilized jar, gently pressing down to ensure that the tomatoes are covered by the juice that has been released.

5. Pour chlorine-free water into the jar to completely cover the tomatoes, leaving about 1 inch (2.5 cm) of headspace at the top of the jar.

6. Cover the jar with a clean cloth or cheesecloth and secure it with a rubber band or plastic tie.

7. Place the jar in a cool place, away from direct sunlight, and let it ferment for 3-5 days. During this period, check the jar periodically to make sure there are no signs of mold or unpleasant odors.

8. After the desired fermentation period, transfer the contents of the jar to a blender or food processor. Add sugar and apple cider vinegar and blend until smooth.

9. Taste the sauce and, if necessary, adjust the flavor by adding a little salt or vinegar.

10. Transfer the fermented tomato sauce to clean and sterilized jars. Store in the refrigerator and consume within 1-2 weeks.

PICKLING

Pickling is a traditional method of preserving the freshness and flavor of vegetables. This technique, dating back to ancient times, relies on the use of vinegar as a preserving agent. Pickling not only extends the shelf life of vegetables but also adds a unique taste and a touch of acidity that makes them irresistible.

During the pickling process, the vegetables are immersed in a solution of vinegar and spices. Vinegar acts as a natural preservative due to its antimicrobial properties, which inhibit the growth of bacteria and fungi responsible for food spoilage. The addition of spices such as garlic, chili, and mustard gives the vegetables an aromatic and spicy flavor, further enhancing the taste experience.

SUITABLE FOODS
1. Vegetables (e.g., cucumbers, onions, peppers)
2. Mushrooms
3. Olives
4. Eggs
5. Chili peppers
6. Roots (e.g., radish, carrots, beets)
7. Citrus fruits (e.g., lemons)
8. Dairy products (e.g., pickled cheeses)

UNSUITABLE FOODS
1. Fresh meats (e.g., beef, pork, poultry)
2. Fresh fish
3. Fresh milk
4. Fresh fruits (except for some varieties used in specific fermentations)
5. High-sugar foods (e.g., candies, chocolate)
6. Foods with added chemical preservatives (e.g., industrially packaged products)

MATERIALS NEEDED

- **Sharp knife:** A well-sharpened knife will help you cut the vegetables precisely and evenly.

- **Cutting board:** Use a clean and sturdy cutting board to slice the vegetables without damaging your work surfaces.

- **Airtight glass jars with lids:** Clean glass jars with airtight lids are essential for safely and durably storing pickled vegetables.

- **Jar sterilizing pot (optional):** If you want to ensure optimal preservation, a pot for sterilizing jars will allow you to create a bacteria-free environment.

- **Funnel:** The funnel will help you pour the pickling liquid and vegetables into the jars without spills or mess.

- **Bowl:** Use a bowl to prepare and mix the necessary ingredients for pickling.

- **Pot for boiling water:** A pot for boiling water will be useful for preparing the pickling liquid and sterilizing utensils.

- **Tongs for removing vegetables from the pickling liquid:** Tongs will allow you to retrieve the pickled vegetables without contaminating the liquid or damaging the ingredients.

- **Permanent marker:** Use a permanent marker to label the jars with the type of vegetable and the pickling date.

- **Labels:** Labels will help you easily identify the contents of the jars, avoiding confusion or loss.

PROCEDURE
1. Ingredient preparation:
  - Thoroughly wash the fresh vegetables and remove any unwanted parts.
  - Cut the vegetables into pieces or slices of the desired size.
2. Jar preparation:
  - Clean and sterilize the glass jars along with their respective lids.
  - Ensure the jars are completely dry before use.
3. Pickling liquid preparation:
  - In a pot, bring a mixture of vinegar, water, and salt to a boil. The amount of vinegar depends on personal taste and the specific recipe.
  - Add desired spices and flavors to the pickling liquid. You can use garlic, chili, mustard seeds, bay leaves, or other spices of your choice.
4. Filling the jars:
  - Place the cut ingredients inside the sterilized jars.
  - Pour the boiling pickling liquid into the jars, ensuring that the vegetables are completely covered.
  - Use a funnel to prevent splashes and spills.
5. Sealing and storage:
  - Thoroughly clean the edges of the jars to remove any residue.
  - Seal the jars with the airtight lids and tighten them securely.
  - Label the jars with the type of vegetable and the pickling date.
6. Pickling process:
  - Store the jars in a cool, dark, and dry place.
  - Let the jars rest for at least 2-3 weeks to allow the vegetables to ferment and develop their characteristic flavor.

During the pickling process, it is important to follow proper hygiene and food safety procedures. Always wash your hands before handling the ingredients, clean utensils and work surfaces thoroughly, and ensure that the jars are properly sealed to prevent bacterial contamination.

Once opened, store the jars in the refrigerator and consume the pickled vegetables within a reasonable period of time. Always follow the specific recipe instructions and use fresh, high-quality ingredients to ensure safe and high-quality pickling.

PICKLED CHEESE

PREPARATION TIME
20 MINUTES

FERMENTATION
2-3 WEEKS

INGREDIENTS

- 1 lb of hard cheese (e.g., cheddar, gouda)
- 2 cups of apple cider vinegar
- 2 tablespoons of sugar
- 2 tablespoons of kosher salt
- 2 bay leaves
- 1 teaspoon of black peppercorns

PROCEDURE

1. Cut the cheese into cubes or thin slices and place them in a clean, sterilized jar.

2. In a pot, combine the apple cider vinegar, sugar, kosher salt, bay leaves, and black peppercorns. Bring to a boil and let it simmer for 5 minutes.

3. Pour the hot marinade over the cheese in the jar, making sure it is completely submerged.

4. Seal the jar tightly and let it ferment at room temperature for 2-3 weeks.

5. After fermentation, store the pickled cheese in the refrigerator. It is ready to be consumed after 24 hours, but it will improve with time. It is recommended to consume it within 1-2 months.

PICKLED FRUIT

PREPARATION TIME
30 MINUTES

FERMENTATION
1-2 WEEKS

INGREDIENTS

- 1 lb of fruit of your choice (e.g., apples, pears, peaches)
- 2 cups of white wine vinegar
- 1 cup of sugar
- 1 tablespoon of star anise seeds
- 1 cinnamon stick

PROCEDURE

1. Wash and cut the fruit into pieces or slices, removing any seeds or cores if necessary. Place it in a clean, sterilized jar.

2. In a pot, bring the white wine vinegar and sugar to a boil. Let it simmer for 5 minutes.

3. Add the star anise seeds and cinnamon stick to the hot marinade.

4. Pour the marinade over the fruit in the jar, making sure it is fully covered.

5. Seal the jar tightly and let it ferment at room temperature for 1-2 weeks.

6. After fermentation, store the pickled fruit in the refrigerator. It is ready to be consumed after 24 hours, but it will improve with time. It is recommended to consume it within 1-2 months.

PICKLED CARROTS AND PEPPERS

PREPARATION TIME
30 MINUTES

FERMENTATION
1-2 WEEKS

INGREDIENTS

- 1 lb carrots
- 1 lb peppers
- 2 cups water
- 1 cup white wine vinegar
- 2 tablespoons salt
- 2 tablespoons sugar
- 2 garlic cloves
- 1 teaspoon fennel seeds

PROCEDURE

1. Clean the carrots and cut them into sticks or rounds.
2. Clean the peppers, remove seeds and inner membranes, and cut them into strips.
3. In a pot, bring water, white wine vinegar, salt, sugar, garlic cloves, and fennel seeds to a boil.
4. Remove the pot from the heat and let the mixture cool for a few minutes.
5. Arrange the carrots and peppers in clean glass jars.
6. Pour the hot pickling liquid over the vegetables, ensuring they are fully covered.
7. Seal the jars tightly and let them cool to room temperature.
8. Allow the pickled carrots and peppers to ferment at room temperature for 1-2 weeks, making sure to check the fermentation process daily.
9. After the desired fermentation period, store the pickles in the refrigerator for an additional 24 hours before consuming to allow the flavors to fully develop.

PICKLED CUCUMBERS

PREPARATION TIME
20 MINUTES

FERMENTATION
24 HOURS

INGREDIENTS

- 2 lb fresh cucumbers
- 2 cups water
- 1 cup apple cider vinegar
- 2 tablespoons salt
- 2 tablespoons sugar
- 2 teaspoons mustard seeds
- 2 bay leaves
- 1 teaspoon whole peppercorns

PROCEDURE

1. Thoroughly wash the cucumbers and remove the ends.
2. Slice the cucumbers thinly or leave them whole, depending on your preference.
3. In a pot, bring water, apple cider vinegar, salt, sugar, mustard seeds, bay leaves, and peppercorns to a boil.
4. Remove the pot from the heat and let the mixture cool for a few minutes.
5. Arrange the cucumbers in clean glass jars.
6. Pour the hot pickling liquid over the cucumbers, ensuring they are fully submerged.
7. Seal the jars tightly and let them cool to room temperature.
8. Store the pickled cucumbers in the refrigerator for at least 24 hours before consuming to allow the flavors to develop.

PICKLED GREEN BEANS

PREPARATION TIME
30 MINUTES

FERMENTATION
1-2 WEEKS

INGREDIENTS

- 1 lb fresh green beans
- 2 cups water
- 1 cup white wine vinegar
- 2 tablespoons salt
- 2 tablespoons sugar
- 2 garlic cloves
- 1 teaspoon mustard seeds
- 1 teaspoon fennel seeds

PROCEDURE

1. Clean the green beans, removing the ends and any strings.

2. In a pot, bring water, white wine vinegar, salt, sugar, garlic cloves, mustard seeds, and fennel seeds to a boil.

3. Remove the pot from the heat and let the mixture cool for a few minutes.

4. Arrange the green beans in clean glass jars.

5. Pour the hot pickling liquid over the green beans, ensuring they are fully covered.

6. Seal the jars tightly and let them cool to room temperature.

7. Allow the pickled green beans to ferment at room temperature for 1-2 weeks, checking the fermentation process regularly.

8. After the desired fermentation period, store the pickles in the refrigerator for an additional 24 hours before consuming.

SPICED PICKLED CAULIFLOWER

PREPARATION TIME
30 MINUTES

FERMENTATION
1-2 WEEKS

INGREDIENTS

- 1 lb cauliflower
- 2 cups water
- 1 cup white wine vinegar
- 2 tablespoons salt
- 2 tablespoons sugar
- 2 garlic cloves
- 1 teaspoon mustard seeds
- 1 teaspoon fennel seeds
- 1 teaspoon dried red chili flakes (optional)

PROCEDURE

1. Break the cauliflower into small florets.

2. In a pot, bring water, white wine vinegar, salt, sugar, garlic cloves, mustard seeds, fennel seeds, and dried red chili flakes (if desired) to a boil.

3. Remove the pot from the heat and let the mixture cool for a few minutes.

4. Arrange the cauliflower florets in clean glass jars.

5. Pour the hot pickling liquid over the cauliflower, ensuring it is fully covered.

6. Seal the jars tightly and let them cool to room temperature.

7. Allow the spiced pickled cauliflower to ferment at room temperature for 1-2 weeks, checking the fermentation process regularly.

8. After the desired fermentation period, store the pickles in the refrigerator for an additional 24 hours before consuming.

CONCLUSION

Throughout the cookbook, a wide range of meat canning methods has been addressed. These methods offer a practical solution for reducing waste and maximizing our food supply. By implementing the suggested practices, readers can now have a steady stockpile of canned meats in their pantry or to gift to their friends and family, perfect for any occasion or emergency.

The book delves into the advantages of meat canning and its positive impact on one's lifestyle by helping save time, money, and resources. Furthermore, it systematically breaks down critical steps—from selecting quality meats, adhering to safe handling procedures, and choosing appropriate preservation techniques like pressure cooking—to ensure a successful process.

One noteworthy aspect of this cookbook is its attention to detail in providing thoroughly tested recipes, incorporating a variety of meats along with delicious flavors and spices. The recipes guarantee every reader will find something that caters to their personal taste buds—from delectable Asian Chicken Thighs to hearty Beef Stew or exotic venison dishes.

To summarize, the "**Meat Canning Cookbook**" is an indispensable guide that equips readers with comprehensive knowledge, skills, and tasty recipes to preserve meats at home successfully. Its practical and engaging approach simplifies this seemingly complex art form allowing anyone to become a seasoned meat canner, reaping the benefits of sustainability and self-sufficiency while enjoying gourmet delicacies.

INDEX

Sun-Dried Tomato & Basil Turkey Meatballs, 50
Sweet and Sour Chicken, 45
Swiss Steak with Tomato Gravy, 30
Tender Beef Bourguignon, 24
Teriyaki Glazed Quail, 74
Teriyaki Sauce, 108
Teriyaki-Glazed Sliced Sirloin Steak, 18
Thai Red Curry Duck, 75
Tomato Sauce, 106
Traditional Pork and Beans, 70
Turkey and Green Beans, 53
Turkey Bone Broth, 99
Turkey Stroganoff, 52
Vegetable Broth, 102
Venison Stew, 83
White Chicken Chili, 41
Wild Duck Curry, 77

Printed in the USA
CPSIA information can be obtained
at www.ICGtesting.com
LVHW071634020224
770787LV00003B/369